MW00717008

Under the Sun and
in the Kingdom

Under the Sun and in the Kingdom

A Devotional Commentary on Ecclesiastes

Edward B. Allen

Melbourne

Under the Sun and in the Kingdom: A Devotional Commentary on Ecclesiastes
by Edward B. Allen
Copyright © 2020 by Edward B. Allen
All rights reserved worldwide.
Reprinted with revisions, 2021.

Published by Edward B. Allen
Melbourne, Florida
Email: edward.allen1949@gmail.com

ISBN: 978-1-7333042-4-5 (paperback)
978-1-7333042-5-2 (ebook *.epub)
978-1-7333042-6-9 (Kindle ebook *.mobi)

Contact the publisher if you have questions regarding copying this book.

Unless otherwise noted, all Scripture quotations are taken from the *Christian Standard Bible*® (marked CSB ®), Copyright © 2020 by Holman Bible Publishers. Used by permission. The *Christian Standard Bible*® and CSB ® are federally registered trademarks of Holman Bible Publishers.

Scriptures quoted in this work are noted by the following abbreviations and follow usage guidelines of each publisher.

CSB, *Christian Standard Bible*, © 2020 Holman Bible Publishers
KJV, *The Holy Bible*, King James Version, pubic domain

Cover design by Ken Raney (http://kenraney.com). The cover photo is of "The Thinker" by Auguste Rodin.

To Angie

Contents

Contents

Preface

What has lasting value in life? Philosophers through the centuries have sought to answer this question. They have proposed many answers. The book of Ecclesiastes in the Bible addresses this question. It considers many aspects of life and offers a universal message for anyone who lives "under the sun."

Jesus Christ offers forgiveness of sin and life in the Kingdom of God. The New Testament explains what this means. A Christian's life simultaneously runs on these two tracks, ordinary life under the sun like everyone else and life in the Kingdom of God.

Instead of analyzing philosophy, this book presents practical applications of the message of Ecclesiastes and the Kingdom of God. This book consists of passage-by-passage devotional comments on Ecclesiastes and relevant passages in the New Testament. The personal stories are based on the recollections of actual people and events by friends, family, or myself unless otherwise indicated.

You may also want to read traditional commentaries which address other concerns, such as textual variants of manuscripts, translation issues, cultural context, and alternative interpretations. Even though this is not an academic book, I have benefited greatly from Christian scholars. Some word translations, cultural notes, and interpretations come from commentaries by J. Stafford Wright[1] and Benjamin Shaw[2] who are evangelical Bible scholars. I hope you will read their commentaries for yourself. The *UBS Old Testament Handbook* has also been helpful.[3] Unfortunately, it is not practical to cite all the pastors and books from whom I have gleaned over the years.

The Christian Standard Bible (CSB) is quoted as the primary translation. It is a modern translation based on the latest evangelical Bible scholarship. There are a few quotes from the King James Version (KJV) as well. Clarifications of quotations are in [brackets]. Scripture references consist of book, chapter, verses, and version (if relevant), for example, "John 3:16 (KJV)." When Ecclesiastes is referenced, the book is omitted, for example, "3:1 (CSB)."

A word or phrase referred to as a word is in *italics*. Male pronouns are some-

---

[1] J. Stafford Wright, "Ecclesiastes," *The Expositor's Bible Commentary: Psalms–Song of Songs*, Vol. 5 (Grand Rapids, Michigan: Zondervan, 1991).

[2] Benjamin Shaw, *Ecclesiastes: Life in a Fallen World* (Carlisle, Pennsylvania: Banner of Truth Trust, 2019).

[3] *UBS Old Testament Handbook* (United Bible Societies, 2004).

times used to indicate a person of either gender. Transliterated Hebrew words are also in *italics*, mostly in notes. Hebrew definitions are from Strong's *Exhaustive Concordance of the Bible* unless otherwise indicated. Strong's reference numbers for Hebrew words are used rather than full citations, for example, "(*Strong's* No. 1892)." Addresses of Web sites are followed by dates when they were valid, for example, "(Current November 1, 2020)." All Scripture references and section titles are indexed.

I thank Linda Rogers and Mike Constantine for their helpful comments. I am also thankful for the steadfast support of my wife, Angie.

E.B.A.

1

Under the sun

The mid-day sun was hot. I was hoping for some shade from a little cloud as I pulled weeds. The weeds like the sun's light just like the flowers and vegetables. Like the plants, I do my work while the sun makes its trek across the sky. I live under the sun.

> The words of the Preacher, the son of David, king in Jerusalem.
> Vanity of vanities, saith the Preacher, vanity of vanities; all is vanity.
> What profit hath a man of all his labour which he taketh under the sun?
>
> Ecclesiastes 1:1–3 (KJV)

When a Christian starts reading Ecclesiastes, the first reaction is "This sure is negative and discouraging." Many give up after reading these first few verses. The author was searching for lasting value in life. His rhetorical question "What profit has a man?" implies he found nothing.

Ecclesiastes uses the phrase *under the sun* to describe life in general for people on earth. Even though it is part of the Old Testament, the message is not limited to ancient Israel, but it applies to everyone.

The first time I read Ecclesiastes was as homework for a high-school Philosophy class. Ecclesiastes is one of the oldest statements of philosophy in world literature.

> Be careful that no one takes you captive through philosophy and empty deceit based on human tradition, based on the elements of the world, rather than Christ.
>
> Colossians 2:8 (CSB)

This verse in Colossians made me distinguish the philosophies of human traditions in my Philosophy class from what the Bible teaches. Because Ecclesiastes is in the Bible, I learned some godly philosophy.

> Now without faith it is impossible to please God, since the one who
> draws near to him must believe that he exists and that he rewards
> those who seek him.
>
> Hebrews 11:6 (CSB)

Life as a Christian is based on faith and starts with believing God exists
and seeking a relationship with him. Pleasing the Creator gives purpose and
meaning to life.

Atheists live only under the sun. They only see this physical world and
human relationships. They are unaware of the rewards that come with a relationship with the Creator of the universe.

Two tracks

A train runs on two parallel rails. They guide the wheels to wherever it is
supposed to go.

Life for a Christian runs on two simultaneous tracks, ordinary daily life
and life in the Kingdom of God. Studying Ecclesiastes gives one insight into
the under-the-sun track, and related passages from the New Testament yield
insight into the Kingdom track.

My under-the-sun track includes my job, shopping, cleaning, taking out the
garbage, yard work, and home maintenance. There's nothing very glamorous
in that list. Entertainment, hobbies, sports, and birthday parties are also under
the sun. Will Ecclesiastes tell me which of these things has lasting value?

> Let us hear the conclusion of the whole matter: Fear God, and
> keep his commandments: for this is the whole duty of man. For
> God shall bring every work into judgment, with every secret thing,
> whether it be good, or whether it be evil.
>
> Ecclesiastes 12:13–14 (KJV)

These last two verses of Ecclesiastes reveal the conclusion of the author's
search for meaning and lasting value in life under the sun, namely, obey God's
commandments and remember that God will hold one accountable for everything one does. Even though the author found most of life under the sun to
be vanity, he concluded that reverence for God and awareness of his justice are
important.

The author's conclusion about life under the sun motivates me to seek a
deeper understanding of what God expects of me and what his justice involves.
The New Testament is my guide for living in the Kingdom.

> Jesus replied, "Truly I tell you, unless someone is born again, he
> cannot see the kingdom of God."
>
> "How can anyone be born when he is old?" Nicodemus asked
> him. "Can he enter his mother's womb a second time and be born?"

2

> Jesus answered, "Truly I tell you, unless someone is born of water and the Spirit, he cannot enter the kingdom of God."
>
> John 3:3–5 (CSB)

Living under the sun does not require special qualifications. Everyone is born of water during natural childbirth when the mother's water breaks, so everyone lives under the sun.

To also live in the Kingdom, one must enter the Kingdom of God. Jesus said entering happens when one is born of the Spirit—a born-again experience. I had that born-again experience when I was ten years old. I repented of my sins and asked God to come into my life. It was a simple act of faith. I became a citizen of the Kingdom of God.

The New Testament explains how to live in the Kingdom. As one studies Ecclesiastes passage by passage, one finds there are New Testament Scriptures about the Kingdom that are related to life under the sun.

Outline

Outlines benefit modern readers by helping us remember the main points. Writers in ancient times did not use outlines, chapters and verses, or headings; they just organized their material as they saw fit. The organization is implied by the words. Bible commentators often have different outlines of Ecclesiastes which reflect their emphases and interpretations. Ecclesiastes includes narrative prose, poetry, and many proverbs. The outline below is my opinion.[1]

The first level of this outline consists of major sections. About half of these major sections end with a passage recommending that one enjoy life under the sun in spite of its vanity. That indicates another major section follows.

The second level of this outline consists of specific points or illustrations, often at the paragraph level. The beginning and end of distinct passages are marked by literary structure and changes in subject matter. Many passages begin with a personal action, such as "I saw," "I observed," "I said," "I knew," or a similar phrase. Many passages end declaring the previous scene was vanity. Some passages end with one or two proverbs.

---

1. Prologue 1:1–11

    a. Author 1:1

    b. Vanity 1:2–3

    c. Nothing new 1:4–11

        i. Cycles of creation 1:4–7

        ii. Cycles of human history 1:8–11

---

[1] The outline here differs from the outline embedded in the *Christian Standard Bible,* which is the primary translation used by this book. Quoted passages may have paragraphs according to my outline.

2

Prologue

What is Ecclesiastes all about? What is the conclusion? The first and last major sections are a prologue and an epilogue of the book. The Prologue introduces the overall topic of Ecclesiastes and the Epilogue presents the conclusions. The emphatic declarations of "Vanity"[1] tie these sections together.

Ecclesiastes 1:1 (CSB)

1 The words of the Teacher, son of David, king in Jerusalem.

Tradition says King Solomon was the author of Ecclesiastes. Even though scholars may debate date and authorship, this tradition is sufficient for this study.[2] The author gave himself the title *Teacher* (CSB),[3] which we use in this study.

Ecclesiastes describes life in a land with a stable economy and government, such as during Solomon's reign. Life in a war-torn country or in perennial famine has other considerations.

Vanity

As the plane ascended, it was obvious from my window seat the clouds were not balls of cotton. They melted away as we went through them. Water vapor doesn't have any substance.

---

[1] 1:2 and 12:8.

[2] Shaw, pp. 1–4.

[3] The Hebrew word *qohelet* (*Strong's* No. 6953). The precise meaning of this Hebrew word is uncertain, so you may notice different titles in various Bible translations. The Septuagint (Greek) Old Testament translated this Hebrew word as *ekklesiastes* (1:12) from which we get the name of the book, *Ecclesiastes*.

The Hebrew word translated *vanity*[4] by the KJV literally means a vapor.[5] The word is used figuratively, so the CSB translates it as *futility*. The word has a variety of meanings elsewhere in the Old Testament and among English translations of Ecclesiastes.[6] This study uses the word *vanity* because the KJV translation is so familiar, but CSB quotations here declare *futility*.

Ecclesiastes 1:2–3 (CSB)

---

2 "Absolute futility," says the Teacher.
"Absolute futility. Everything is futile."
3 What does a person gain for all his efforts
that he labors at under the sun?

These first few verses of Ecclesiastes present the question the Teacher was trying to answer and his frustration with what he saw.[7]

Under the sun. Daily life entails work. Just acquiring the basics of food, clothing, and shelter takes effort. A job is necessary to earn enough money. There are errands to do. There are bills to pay. There are chores to do. Pulling weeds in the backyard is not my favorite pastime.

The Teacher's overarching quest was to find lasting value in what is done in life.[8] When he exclaimed that everything is vanity, he was hinting that perhaps under the sun the answer is nothing has lasting value. The rest of Ecclesiastes explains why he felt this way.

I wonder whether my chores are really valuable in the long run. I do my chores to manage daily life, but the benefits are temporary. I have errands to do tomorrow, and I'm still looking for something to kill crabgrass. I live under the sun.

In the Kingdom. After I became a Christian believer, I gradually learned from the Bible what life as a citizen of the Kingdom entails. Just knowing what the Bible says is not enough. Putting the Scriptures into practice has been a lifelong journey.

Jesus said to his disciples, "If anyone wants to follow after me, let him deny himself, take up his cross, and follow me."

Matthew 16:24 (CSB)

People in the world work hard to get rich and achieve success. Living in the Kingdom means giving up selfish desires and goals and embracing God's

---

[4]The Hebrew word *hebel* (*Strong's* No. 1892).

[5]Shaw, p. 6.

[6]For example, the *UBS Old Testament Handbook, s.v.* 1:1–11, suggests translating *hebel* in Ecclesiastes as incomprehensible, enigmatic, mysterious, or impossible to understand.

[7]Wright, pp. 1151–1152, emphasizes *frustration* as the theme of Ecclesiastes.

[8]*UBS Old Testament Handbook, s.v.* 1:1–11.

definition of success. Living in the Kingdom seems like a death sentence in the eyes of the world. Living in the Kingdom means following Jesus.

> Brothers and sisters, I do not consider myself to have taken hold of [perfection]. But one thing I do: Forgetting what is behind and reaching forward to what is ahead, I pursue as my goal the prize promised by God's heavenly call in Christ Jesus.
>
> Philippians 3:13–14 (CSB)

The Teacher was seeking lasting value, but couldn't find any in life under the sun. Paul was also seeking lasting value, but he was pursuing a heavenly prize. His goal was to know Christ and his resurrection power. He had not yet achieved perfection. He did not let his past interfere with his quest. He was striving to fulfill God's purpose in life in the Kingdom.

An athlete must concentrate on the task before him and not be bothered by his mistakes in the past. For example, a baseball pitcher must not worry over how the previous pitch missed its target, and a batter must not fret over the previous swing that missed the ball. They both must concentrate on the next pitch.

I am determined to follow Paul's example. I will not be distracted by my past failures which have all been forgiven. I will concentrate on getting to know Jesus better each day and to please him, because I live in the Kingdom.

Nothing new

Thomas Edison (1847–1931) was a consummate inventor. He was credited with over a thousand US patents. An early electric light bulb is perhaps his most famous invention. However, even though amazing technologies may be invented, human behavior is basically the same generation after generation.

This passage is poetry in two parts: nature repeats cycles endlessly; and similarly, people do the same things endlessly, so there is nothing new and memorable that people do.

Ecclesiastes 1:4–7 (CSB)

---

4 A generation goes and a generation comes,
but the earth remains forever.
5 The sun rises and the sun sets;
panting, it hurries back to the place
where it rises.
6 Gusting to the south,
turning to the north,
turning, turning, goes the wind,
and the wind returns in its cycles.
7 All the streams flow to the sea,
yet the sea is never full;

to the place where the streams flow,
there they flow again.

This part of the poem illustrates creation's cycles with three examples: the sun's daily journey in the sky, the wind's seasonal rotation, and how rivers flow to the sea and are constantly supplied by springs. Today, we understand how water returns in clouds and rain to refresh the headwaters of rivers and the aquifers of springs.

Ecclesiastes 1:8–11 (CSB)

---

8 All things are wearisome,
more than anyone can say.
The eye is not satisfied by seeing
or the ear filled with hearing.
9 What has been is what will be,
and what has been done is what will be done;
there is nothing new under the sun.
10 Can one say about anything,
"Look, this is new"?
It has already existed in the ages before us.
11 There is no remembrance of those who came before;
and of those who will come after
there will also be no remembrance
by those who follow them.

This part of the poem considers what people do. The Teacher grew weary looking for something significant.

Under the sun. The cycles of nature seem to never stop. The sun appears to move across the sky, disappears in the West, and reappears in the East. It is even more amazing to realize a globe is actually spinning in space. The cycles of weather are so intricate science barely understands them. The cycles in human history are obvious, too. Technological discoveries may be new, but human behavior is just like the past.

The Teacher saw that God has set creation in order. Generations of people follow one after another. Everyone has a limited lifespan, but creation endures. Creation's cycles continue over and over no matter what people do.

What has happened in the past will happen again. There is nothing new in human affairs that will be so innovative that succeeding generations will remember who did it. Human discoveries, compared to the works of God, do not yield the lasting value the Teacher was seeking.

I enjoy reading history books, but I find it difficult to remember specifics about famous people. I suspect most kids in History class forget everything immediately after the final exam. Fame doesn't last very long. Studying history reminds me I live under the sun.

In the Kingdom. Atheists today not only claim creation continues without God, they now predict one doom after another for earth, such as nuclear bombs, population explosion, famine everywhere, global warming, disappearing biodiversity, and pandemics.

> Above all, be aware of this: Scoffers will come in the last days scoffing and following their own evil desires, saying, … "All things continue as they have been since the beginning of creation." They deliberately overlook this: By the word of God the heavens came into being long ago and the earth was brought about from water and through water… By the same word, the present heavens and earth are stored up for fire, being kept for the day of judgment and destruction of the ungodly…
> But based on his promise, we wait for new heavens and a new earth, where righteousness dwells.
>
> 2 Peter 3:3–7,13 (CSB)

Scoffers, who live only under the sun, mock God's promises because the cycles of creation seem to continue over and over. But God has plans for this old earth. He has promised to clean out evil, and to provide a new heaven and a new earth.

> But as it is written,
>
> > What no eye has seen, no ear has heard,
> > and no human heart has conceived—
> > God has prepared these things for those who love him.
>
> Now God has revealed these things to us by the Spirit, since the Spirit searches everything, even the depths of God.
>
> 1 Corinthians 2:9–10 (CSB)

The Teacher saw no innovation in life under the sun. But God is the supreme innovator. He has prepared things more wonderful than anyone could imagine for those in the Kingdom. For example, forgiveness of sin through the cross was God's boldest innovation.

As I study the Bible, the Holy Spirit shows me new truths I can apply to my life. For example, the Bible teaches me to be a servant, so when I'm putting away my empty trash can, I can put away my neighbor's can, too. Even little things in life have purpose, because I live in the Kingdom.

3

Exploring through wisdom

If I'm looking for buried treasure, I will need a shovel. I'll need the right tools. The Teacher searched for meaning using wisdom. Wisdom was his tool.

Applying my mind to all under heaven

I like to figure things out. Perhaps my favorite question is "How does it work?" My wife claims if you ask me what time it is, I will tell you how to build a clock.

Ecclesiastes 1:12–15 (CSB)

---

12 I, the Teacher, have been king over Israel in Jerusalem. 13 I applied my mind to examine and explore through wisdom all that is done under heaven. God has given people this miserable task to keep them occupied. 14 I have seen all the things that are done under the sun and have found everything to be futile, a pursuit of the wind.

15 What is crooked cannot be straightened;
what is lacking cannot be counted.

After identifying himself again, the beginning of this passage is marked by the personal action, "I applied my mind." The prose concludes with the declaration that everything is vanity, followed by a proverb which marks the end of the passage. The phrase *under heaven* is synonymous with *under the sun*.

Under the sun. In high school, I learned about logic in my Geometry class. However, logic and the text books in my Philosophy class didn't explain how to find lasting value in life.

The Teacher's methodology for his quest was intellectual inquiry and application of wisdom. His "miserable task" was to understand what has lasting value.[1] Summarizing what follows in Ecclesiastes, he declared it is all vanity. Searching for meaning is like trying to catch the wind. The proverb illustrates the point with two impossible tasks: something like a tree branch that grows curved cannot be straightened; and when you have none, you can't count things.

Like the Teacher, I've always thought clear logical thinking and common sense are good ways to find the truth about something. However, the Teacher was unable to find lasting value. His task seemed impossible. If finding meaning in life was difficult for him, how much more will it be for me? I live under the sun.

In the Kingdom. Most people think worldly wisdom and street smarts are what a person needs to be successful. You have to be ambitious to get ahead. You won't be cheated if you have street smarts.

> Who among you is wise and understanding? By his good conduct he should show that his works are done in the gentleness that comes from wisdom. But if you have bitter envy and selfish ambition in your heart, don't boast and deny the truth. Such wisdom does not come down from above but is earthly, unspiritual, demonic. For where there is envy and selfish ambition, there is disorder and every evil practice. But the wisdom from above is first pure, then peace-loving, gentle, compliant, full of mercy and good fruits, unwavering, without pretense. And the fruit of righteousness is sown in peace by those who cultivate peace.
>
> James 3:13–18 (CSB)

James contrasted worldly wisdom with godly wisdom. Worldly wisdom is motivated by envy and selfish ambition and results in chaos and evil actions. Wisdom from God is pure, peaceful, gentle, cooperative, merciful, steadfast, and honest. Those who have godly wisdom are recognized by their gentle behavior.

Solomon was famous for the wisdom God gave him.[2] The Teacher applied this wisdom to his quest for lasting value, but he only examined life under the sun and found only vanity.

I want my wisdom to reflect the virtues James listed above, such as gentleness and good fruit without hypocrisy. Godly wisdom is the wisdom of the Kingdom. I live in the Kingdom.

Applying my mind to wisdom and folly

If the Teacher lived today, he would deserve a Doctor of Philosophy degree. He had grasped all the wisdom of the sophisticated cultures in his region. However, all that education did not make him happy.

---

[1] *UBS Old Testament Handbook*, s.v. 1:13.
[2] 1 Kings 4:29–34.

Ecclesiastes 1:16–18 (CSB)

---

16 I said to myself, "See, I have amassed wisdom far beyond all those who were over Jerusalem before me, and my mind has thoroughly grasped wisdom and knowledge." 17 I applied my mind to know wisdom and knowledge, madness and folly; I learned that this too is a pursuit of the wind.

18 For with much wisdom is much sorrow;
as knowledge increases, grief increases.

The beginning of this passage is marked by the personal action, "I said to myself." The statement "I applied my mind" parallels the previous passage, tying them together for this major section. The end of the prose is marked by the parallel statement, "This too is a pursuit of the wind," followed by a proverb, like the previous passage.

Under the sun. When I studied computer science, I learned about Gödel's Incompleteness Theorems.[3] His theorems prove there is no consistent set of axioms where an algorithm can list all truths (theorems) about arithmetic of natural numbers. In other words, in such a logical system, there will always be statements about natural numbers that are true but unprovable. Gödel's theorems show that logic alone has limitations. These theorems have inspired analogies in other fields. For example, there are truths about human behavior that are unprovable by psychology and sociology.

The Teacher had sufficient wisdom and knowledge for his task. He carefully thought about "wisdom, knowledge, madness, and folly."[4] He found understanding these was also an impossible task, "pursuit of the wind." The proverb conveys how his pursuit of wisdom made him more discouraged than ever.

The Teacher not only examined the world around him, he examined his intellectual tools of wisdom and knowledge and their opposites, foolish thinking and folly. It's a good idea to make sure your tools are in order.

The Teacher observed things that his wisdom could not understand. His frustration trying to understand wisdom and folly is similar to the frustration of a mathematician trying to design a logic algorithm to prove all truth about natural numbers. Like the Teacher, my intellectual tools are inadequate, too. I live under the sun.

In the Kingdom. Late night debates in my college dorm over religion and life may have quoted the world's famous philosophers. The logic of the arguments was precise. My friends may have been budding intellectuals, but they

---

[3] Kurt Gödel published these two theorems in 1931.
[4] *Madness* refers to foolish thinking, not mental illness. *UBS Old Testament Handbook, s.v.* 1:17.

couldn't solve the world's problems. God has the answer for the world's sin problems. The cross is why sin can be forgiven.

> For the word of the cross is foolishness to those who are perishing, but it is the power of God to us who are being saved. For it is written,
>
>> I will destroy the wisdom of the wise,
>> and I will set aside the intelligence of the intelligent.
>
> Where is the one who is wise? Where is the [scholar]? Where is the debater of this age? Hasn't God made the world's wisdom foolish? For since, in God's wisdom, the world did not know God through wisdom, God was pleased to save those who believe through the foolishness of what is preached. For the Jews ask for signs and the Greeks seek wisdom, but we preach Christ crucified, a stumbling block to the Jews and foolishness to the Gentiles. Yet to those who are called, both Jews and Greeks, Christ is the power of God and the wisdom of God, because God's foolishness is wiser than human wisdom, and God's weakness is stronger than human strength.
>
> 1 Corinthians 1:18–25 (CSB)

Paul explained the reaction of intellectuals in society to the message of Christ crucified for the forgiveness of sin. The Greeks were famous for their philosophers, mathematicians, and orators. The Jews were famous for their Bible scholars. It was inconceivable to them that God would choose to save mankind through someone executed as the lowest criminal—by crucifixion.

The message of the cross is foolishness to the intelligentsia. Yet whoever believes is able to enter the Kingdom of God and to understand the wisdom of God's plan. I live in the Kingdom.

4

Testing pleasure

A modern scientist performs experiments to determine answers to his research questions. Although Philosophy is different from Science, testing may still yield insights. The Teacher wondered whether pleasure would be the answer to his quest for lasting value. So, he decided to do some tests.

Ecclesiastes 2:1–2 (CSB)

---

1 I said to myself, "Go ahead, I will test you with pleasure; enjoy what is good." But it turned out to be futile. 2 I said about laughter, "It is madness," and about pleasure, "What does this accomplish?"

These verses introduce the next major section: testing whether pleasure yields lasting value. The beginning of this passage is marked by the personal action, "I said to myself." The second verse also begins with a personal action, " I said."

Under the sun. I like to tell puns and learn new ones. I even laugh at my own jokes. Everyone else groans. Do puns have lasting value? Probably not.

The Teacher decided to find out whether pleasure has lasting benefit. He told us here at the introduction what he found and gave us the evidence in the following passages. He declared that pleasure turned out to be vanity. His verdict over joyful laughter was it is foolishness. The following passages seek to answer his closing question, "What does [pleasure] accomplish?"

When I choose to do something enjoyable, I'm not looking for lasting value in life, and just like the Teacher, I don't find any. I live under the sun.

In the Kingdom. I like to make lists and categorize things. Suppose I made a list of things I enjoy and evaluated them one by one. Is this item from under the sun or the Kingdom? How much do I love it compared to my heavenly

Father? Things under the sun only have temporary value. The Kingdom has lasting value.

> Do not love the world or the things in the world. If anyone loves the world, the love of the Father is not in him.
>
> 1 John 2:15 (CSB)

Pleasure is one of the main attractions of life under the sun. John warned us not to love the pleasures of this world, but to love God instead. My loves and motives always need adjusting, because I live both under the sun and in the Kingdom.

Testing wine

Many people think getting a "buzz" is the way to enjoy life. Today, alcohol is packaged in many kinds of drinks, such as beer, wine, cocktails, and whiskey. Marijuana and other drugs offer a higher high. Does the pleasure of wine yield lasting value? The Teacher did a test.

Ecclesiastes 2:3 (CSB)

---

3 I explored with my mind the pull of wine on my body—my mind still guiding me with wisdom—and how to grasp folly, until I could see what is good for people to do under heaven during the few days of their lives.

The beginning of this passage is marked by the personal action, "I explored with my mind." The end is marked by the phrase *under heaven* which is a synonym for *under the sun.*

Under the sun. When I was in college, many of my friends frequently got drunk on beer or high on marijuana. I avoided alcohol and drugs in general, but there were a few occasions when I drank a glass of wine too quickly and the world started spinning.

The Teacher got drunk, but he kept his wits about him, so he could evaluate whether the folly of intoxicants has lasting value. I wonder if he had a hangover the next morning.

I found out there is no lasting value in wine. Making the world spin is not lasting value. I live under the sun.

In the Kingdom. When I was about twelve years old, I committed myself to follow Jesus whole heartedly. Shortly after, I started noticing the Holy Spirit talking to me. Reading the Bible became more relevant. I felt his nudges to do this or that. When someone was sharing, I might feel the Holy Spirit say, "This is for you."

Pay careful attention, then, to how you walk—not as unwise people but as wise—making the most of the time, because the days are evil. So don't be foolish, but understand what the Lord's will is. And don't get drunk with wine, which leads to reckless living, but be filled by the Spirit.

Ephesians 5:15–18 (CSB)

The wise Christian gives priority to doing what God wants, because evil permeates society around us. The pleasure of getting drunk is a distraction, interfering with listening to the Holy Spirit. I want to be filled with the Holy Spirit all the time, because I live in the Kingdom.

Testing achievements

Ancient kings liked to build monuments about themselves. Solomon built other things, too, like a palace for his wife[1] and the temple of God. Does the pleasure of building things yield lasting value? The Teacher did a test.

Ecclesiastes 2:4–6 (CSB)

---

4 I increased my achievements. I built houses and planted vineyards for myself. 5 I made gardens and parks for myself and planted every kind of fruit tree in them. 6 I constructed reservoirs for myself from which to irrigate a grove of flourishing trees.

The beginning of this passage is marked by the personal action, "I increased my achievements," followed by a series of personal actions.

Under the sun. My backyard is my great project. My goal is a place that is pleasant to look at and doesn't take much work to maintain. Unfortunately, the weeds think it is a great place to grow their offspring. So you will find me out there pulling weeds and planting beach sunflowers.

As king, the Teacher directed great projects. He tested whether the pleasure of building beautiful places, such as vineyards, gardens, parks, and groves, would have lasting value.

Like the Teacher, I haven't found lasting value among the weeds in my backyard yet. My sunburn proves I live under the sun.

In the Kingdom. High rise condominiums line the beaches of South Florida. People like to live close to the beach with a view of the ocean. When storms come, the surf washes away the sand at the base of the buildings. After years of beach erosion, the surf laps at the foundations of those buildings, but the lighthouse among those condos stands on an ancient reef down below.

---

[1] 1 Kings 7:8.

Therefore, everyone who hears these words of mine and acts on
them will be like a wise man who built his house on the rock. The
rain fell, the rivers rose, and the winds blew and pounded that
house. Yet it didn't collapse, because its foundation was on the
rock. But everyone who hears these words of mine and doesn't
act on them will be like a foolish man who built his house on the
sand. The rain fell, the rivers rose, the winds blew and pounded
that house, and it collapsed. It collapsed with a great crash.

Matthew 7:24–27 (CSB)

Jesus told the parable of the wise man who built his house on rock, and
the foolish man who built his house on sand. The house on sand was swept
away by a storm. The parable of the builders is at the end of the Sermon on the
Mount.[2] The rock represents the entire Sermon on the Mount. Building one's
life on Jesus' teaching is secure like building a house on rock.

When I read the Sermon on the Mount, I see how I must live. Citizens of
the Kingdom are blessed. I must love my enemy. I will pray simple prayers. I
must not worry about my finances. When I ask the Father, he will answer with
good things. I live in the Kingdom.

Testing wealth

Casino slot machines are a popular form of entertainment. There is a celebra-
tion when one wins a jackpot or even a small payout. Does the pleasure of
gaining wealth yield lasting value? The Teacher did a test.

Ecclesiastes 2:7–8 (CSB)

---

7 I acquired male and female servants and had slaves who were
born in my house. I also owned livestock—large herds and flocks—
more than all who were before me in Jerusalem. 8 I also amassed
silver and gold for myself, and the treasure of kings and provinces.
I gathered male and female singers for myself, and many concubines, the delights of men.

This passage consists of a series of personal actions, such as the first one, "I
acquired." The meaning of the Hebrew word translated *concubines*[3] by the CSB
is uncertain.

Under the sun. I bought a sporty car to drive to work. It even had a retractable
sunroof. I parked it among the cars the accountants drove. After a few years,

---

[2]Matthew 5:1–7:29.

[3]The Hebrew word *shiddah* (*Strong's* No. 7705). Shaw, pp. 23–24. Wright, p. 1157. You may
notice wide differences of opinion among Bible translations of verse 8.

the sunroof started to leak. After an afternoon shower, water accumulated inside the ceiling. When I started to pull out of the parking space, a downpour of water emptied the ceiling onto my head.

The Teacher tested whether accumulating wealth would yield lasting value. He acquired all the status symbols of his culture, everything a rich king should have. He was so powerful that kings and governors of distant provinces paid tribute to him.

I guess accumulating status symbols of modern culture isn't alway a good idea, even if I do live under the sun.

In the Kingdom. Whenever I changed jobs there was always a big jump in my salary, sometimes up and sometimes down. God always provided enough for me and my wife, no matter how big or small the paycheck was.

> I don't say this out of need, for I have learned to be content in whatever circumstances I find myself. I know how to make do with little, and I know how to make do with a lot. In any and all circumstances I have learned the secret of being content—whether well fed or hungry, whether in abundance or in need. I am able to do all things through him who strengthens me.
>
> Philippians 4:11–13 (CSB)

Paul testified that he had been content in all kinds of circumstances. He was content when he had abundance. He was content when he had little. Acquiring wealth was not necessary for his success.

Like Paul, I have been content. Wealth is not the measure of success. Contentment is better than a big paycheck, because I live in the Kingdom.

Enjoying life

After performing an experiment, a scientist analyzes his data to determine his results. The Teacher had tested pleasure. This passage summarizes his conclusions.

Ecclesiastes 2:9–11 (CSB)

---

9 So I became great and surpassed all who were before me in Jerusalem; my wisdom also remained with me. 10 All that my eyes desired, I did not deny them. I did not refuse myself any pleasure, for I took pleasure in all my struggles. This was my reward for all my struggles. 11 When I considered all that I had accomplished and what I had labored to achieve, I found everything to be futile and a pursuit of the wind. There was nothing to be gained under the sun.

The beginning of this passage is marked by the personal action, "I became great," followed by a series of other personal actions. The end of this passage is marked by declaring everything is vanity.

Under the sun. I enjoyed seeing beach sunflowers ("dune daisies") grow in my backyard. My sporty car was fun to drive for a while. I still laugh at my own jokes.

The Teacher kept his wisdom, so he could evaluate what has lasting value. As a great king, he enjoyed all the avenues of pleasure he had listed above. "I took pleasure in all my struggles." The enjoyment itself was his only reward for building and acquiring things.

There is some pleasure and beauty in the mundane things of daily life, so I'll enjoy them. I live under the sun.

In the Kingdom. Advertising on TV tells me about all the things I should want. "Sex sells," "Beer satisfies," and "Cars are fun." Should I pay attention to the ads?

> For everything in the world—the lust of the flesh, the lust of the eyes, and the pride in one's possessions—is not from the Father, but is from the world. And the world with its lust is passing away, but the one who does the will of God remains forever.
>
> 1 John 2:16–17 (CSB)

Feeling good, pleasant surroundings, and pride lead one to think life under the sun is significant, but this world is just temporary. Life in the Kingdom is eternal.

Worldly desires are temptations which try to distract me from the Kingdom. Fulfilling such desires may feel good at the moment, but doing what God wants produces lasting value. I live in the Kingdom.

5

Comparing wisdom and folly

Wisdom or folly—which is better? Which offers lasting benefit? Is a wise person better off than a fool?

Walking in light

After the Boy-Scout campfire ceremony was over, we had to walk through the woods to get to our tents. One guy remembered to bring a flashlight. A bunch of us followed him.

Ecclesiastes 2:12–14 (CSB)

---

12 Then I turned to consider wisdom, madness, and folly, for what will the king's successor be like? He will do what has already been done. 13 And I realized that there is an advantage to wisdom over folly, like the advantage of light over darkness.

14 The wise person has eyes in his head,
but the fool walks in darkness.

The beginning of this passage is marked by the personal action, "I turned to consider wisdom." The end is marked by a proverb.

Under the sun. The night before final exams, some of my friends had a party, got drunk, and stayed up into the wee hours of the morning. I guess they gave up on getting decent grades. I thought studying and getting a good night's sleep was a better final-exam strategy. However, all the noise in the dorm made it hard to sleep.

In this passage, the Teacher compared wisdom and folly.[1] He concluded that wisdom is better than folly, because the wise person is aware of his surrounding like one walking in a lighted area.

When in school, studying is better than parties, because wisdom is better than folly. Common sense helps me avoid tripping in awkward situations. I live under the sun.

In the Kingdom. One moonless night, the power went out all over town.[2] It was dark everywhere. There were dark houses, dark porches, dark streets, dark businesses. We felt relief when the power came back on.

> [God] has rescued us from the domain of darkness and transferred us into the kingdom of the Son he loves. In him we have redemption, the forgiveness of sins.
>
> Colossians 1:13–14 (CSB)

The domain of sin is like darkness. Jesus' Kingdom is the opposite. God has forgiven my sins so I am no longer walking in darkness. Like when the lights came on, I felt relief when God transferred me from the domain of sin. Now, I live in the Kingdom.

Death of the wise and the fool

Two eighteen year-old guys died when their truck hit a tree. A college professor died of cancer. Who had gained lasting value under the sun?

Ecclesiastes 2:14–16 (CSB)

Yet I also knew that one fate comes to them both. 15 So I said to myself, "What happens to the fool will also happen to me. Why then have I been overly wise?" And I said to myself that this is also futile.

16 For, just like the fool, there is no lasting remembrance of the wise, since in the days to come both will be forgotten. How is it that the wise person dies just like the fool?

The beginning of this passage is marked by the personal actions, "Yet I also knew," and "So I said to myself." The section ends with a question which is left unanswered.

---

[1] The Teacher was also concerned whether his heir will be wise or foolish, but this point is discussed more later.

[2] A squirrel was electrocuted at a substation.

Under the sun. I spent over twenty years going to school. I learned many things that helped me during my career, but the results of my career will fade away. I can't think of anything I learned in school that will benefit me after I die.

Even though wisdom is better than folly, everyone dies. The Teacher had expended considerable effort acquiring wisdom and knowledge, but he concluded, because of death, acquiring wisdom is also vanity. Neither wisdom nor folly guarantees anyone will remember a person after he has died.

I won't be remembered after I die. Someone may read this book after I die, but this book will be forgotten, too. Acquired wisdom is just temporary. I live under the sun.

In the Kingdom. We grieve when a loved one dies. It doesn't matter whether the deceased was wise or foolish; he was loved. Everyone dies, but I have a solid hope for my resurrection, because Jesus conquered death.

> We do not want you to be uninformed, brothers and sisters, concerning those who are asleep, so that you will not grieve like the rest, who have no hope. For if we believe that Jesus died and rose again, in the same way, through Jesus, God will bring with him those who have fallen asleep.
>
> 1 Thessalonians 4:13–14 (CSB)

People may forget about the wise person and the fool, but God knows all those who belong to him who have died, who are "asleep." When Jesus returns to earth, the dead in Christ will be resurrected to meet Jesus in the air.

I want my funeral to explain my hope, which will comfort the grieving. I will be resurrected when Jesus returns to earth, because I live in the Kingdom.

Hating life

My sand castle at the beach was awesome. It had walls and towers. Pretty soon it was high tide. The waves attacked my castle. A little mound of sand was all that was left.

Ecclesiastes 2:17 (CSB)

---

17 Therefore, I hated life because the work that was done under the sun was distressing to me. For everything is futile and a pursuit of the wind.

This passage completes the major section comparing wisdom and folly. The beginning of this passage is marked by the personal action, "Therefore, I hated life." The end is marked by declaring everything is vanity and chasing the wind.

Under the sun. After working for government contractors for about eight years, I realized the corruption I was seeing was ruining the work we were doing. There was one failed project after another. What would I do next? I ended up changing jobs to work for a health-care company. The results there were still just temporary.

The Teacher considered wisdom better than folly, but death proves neither has lasting value. He was depressed by this realization, and so he hated life and all the work he had invested. Hating life is the opposite of his advice elsewhere to enjoy life. He concluded all is vanity and finding lasting value in wisdom is impossible.

I sympathize with the Teacher. Even though wisdom is better than folly, it is discouraging to realize wisdom does not have lasting value. I worked on many projects during my career. Some were successful and some were failures. All were temporary, because I live under the sun.

In the Kingdom. Eating and drinking are necessary elements of life. I like to eat and drink. I like some kosher food, too, but not gefilte fish. I'd rather have German chocolate cake.

> For the kingdom of God is not eating and drinking, but righteousness, peace, and joy in the Holy Spirit.
>
> Romans 14:17 (CSB)

Life in the Kingdom is not about acting religious and eating kosher cooking. Life in the Kingdom consists of experiencing righteousness, peace, and joy. Life in the Kingdom is embraced, not hated.

I may do religious things at church sometimes, but the essence of life is inside me: knowing my sins are forgiven, sensing quiet in my soul, and feeling happy in spite of my circumstances. I live in the Kingdom.

6

Working

What makes work worth doing? Will an inheritance be handled properly? Is there lasting value in what I have accomplished?

Despair about work

When I moved out of state, my housemates had to do the chores I had been doing around our rental house. I had no idea whether they did a good job or not.

Ecclesiastes 2:18–23 (CSB)

---

18 I hated all my work that I labored at under the sun because I must leave it to the one who comes after me. 19 And who knows whether he will be wise or a fool? Yet he will take over all my work that I labored at skillfully under the sun. This too is futile.

20 So I began to give myself over to despair concerning all my work that I had labored at under the sun. 21 When there is a person whose work was done with wisdom, knowledge, and skill, and he must give his portion to a person who has not worked for it, this too is futile and a great wrong.

22 For what does a person get with all his work and all his efforts that he labors at under the sun? 23 For all his days are filled with grief, and his occupation is sorrowful; even at night, his mind does not rest. This too is futile.

The beginning of this passage is marked by the personal action, "I hated all my work." The second paragraph also begins with a personal action, "So I began to give myself over to despair." Each of the three paragraphs ends declaring this too is vanity.

Under the sun. After working some years in industry, I decided to go back to school. I had to pass on to my coworkers all the things I had been working on. Some projects were complete and some not. I had no control over what would happen to those projects or who would work on them. Would they still benefit the company and its customers? At a going-away luncheon, the company gave me a nice pen and notebook set, but it certainly did not have lasting value.

The Teacher was worried, because he couldn't tell whether his heir would be wise or foolish when he takes over the inheritance. This situation is vanity.

He became even more depressed when he thought about all the effort he had invested and how the results will go to someone who had not worked for it. This situation seemed unfair and is also vanity.

In the third paragraph,[1] the Teacher paraphrased his original question at the beginning of Ecclesiastes,[2] "What does a person get for all his work?" What has lasting value? When one works all the time, even sleep is occupied with worries. This situation is also vanity.

All my accumulated projects will pass to someone when I die. I won't have any control at that point, and I won't need to worry about them at night either. I live under the sun.

In the Kingdom. As a single guy, I accumulated the usual set of kitchen stuff. When my mother died, I inherited all her dishes, pots, pans, and implements. When I married, my wife had most of those items already. So we were equipped for at least three kitchens.

> Don't store up for yourselves treasures on earth, where moth and rust destroy and where thieves break in and steal. But store up for yourselves treasures in heaven, where neither moth nor rust destroys, and where thieves don't break in and steal. For where your treasure is, there your heart will be also.
>
> Matthew 6:19–21 (CSB)

Jesus advised his disciples to focus on treasures in heaven instead of physical possessions. Moths, rust, and thieves ruin possessions under the sun. Treasures in heaven are indestructible. The goal is not to accumulate treasures, but is a heart focused on heavenly things, like righteousness, peace, and joy.

Instead of trying to convert pots and pans into money at a yard sale, we gave away the extras. We were thankful to have even one set of kitchen stuff. I live in the Kingdom.

Enjoying life

Even though there were twists and turns in my career path, God blessed me with an enjoyable career. Of course, any job has ups and downs, but I'm thankful for the ups.

---

[1] 2:22.
[2] 1:3. *UBS Old Testament Handbook, s.v.* 2:22.

Ecclesiastes 2:24–26 (CSB)

---

24 There is nothing better for a person than to eat, drink, and enjoy his work. I have seen that even this is from God's hand, 25 because who can eat and who can enjoy life apart from him? 26 For to the person who is pleasing in his sight, he gives wisdom, knowledge, and joy; but to the sinner he gives the task of gathering and accumulating in order to give to the one who is pleasing in God's sight. This too is futile and a pursuit of the wind.

This passage about enjoying work marks the end of this major section. The beginning of this passage is marked by "There is nothing better." The end of the passage is marked by declaring this too is vanity, like the previous paragraphs, and chasing the wind.

Under the sun. I am an engineer by training. Engineers like to build things. For example, the toilet-paper dispenser came off the wall. I analyzed the situation like any engineer would and then fixed it.

The Teacher recommended enjoying one's work. However, the ability to enjoy work is a gift from God. Wisdom, knowledge, and joy are gifts from God. So, one should live a life that is pleasing to him. However, this did not fulfill the Teacher's quest for lasting value, so enjoying one's work is also vanity and chasing the wind.

God gives me the ability to enjoy the process of building something and seeing a completed project. I'm thankful for that, but I know my toilet-paper dispenser won't last forever. Someday a new one will have to replace the worn out one. I live under the sun.

In the Kingdom. Knowledge in the Kingdom is not about issues like how to fix my broken toilet-paper dispenser. Knowing God through a personal relationship is more important.

> I pray that the God of our Lord Jesus Christ, the glorious Father, would give you the Spirit wisdom and revelation in the knowledge of him. I pray that the eyes of your heart may be enlightened so that you may know what is the hope of his calling, what is the wealth of his glorious inheritance in the saints, and what is the immeasurable greatness of his power toward us who believe, according to the mighty working of his strength.
>
> Ephesians 1:17–19 (CSB)

Paul prayed for those in Ephesus to received wisdom and knowledge from God. He prayed God would reveal himself to them. He prayed for understanding in several areas: the hope of God's calling, the inheritance of God's people, and God's power on behalf of believers.

My heavenly Father helped me figure out my broken toilet-paper dispenser, but he also reveals to me what is important in life: knowing about my purpose, knowing about my inheritance with other believers, and knowing about God's power working on my behalf. I pray for the same understanding that Paul prayed for, both for myself and for fellow believers. I live in the Kingdom.

7

Time and eternity

Seasons in nature cycle through the year. Seasons in human affairs also cycle. When is the right time for a mundane task? When is the right time to find eternal value?

Seasons

I think the four seasons in my Florida are "nice and sunny," "love-bugs," "hot and muggy," and "hurricanes." I'm sure you can think of special seasons where you live that only local residents will understand.

Ecclesiastes 3:1–8 (CSB)

---

1 There is an occasion for everything,
and a time for every activity under heaven:
2 a time to give birth and a time to die;
a time to plant and a time to uproot;
3 a time to kill and a time to heal;
a time to tear down and a time to build;
4 a time to weep and a time to laugh;
a time to mourn and a time to dance;
5 a time to throw stones and a time to gather stones;
a time to embrace and a time to avoid embracing;
6 a time to search and a time to count as lost;
a time to keep and a time to throw away;
7 a time to tear and a time to sew;
a time to be silent and a time to speak;
8 a time to love and a time to hate;
a time for war and a time for peace.

This passage is a poem about seasons of life. It is perhaps the most famous passage in Ecclesiastes, due to the popular song, "Turn! Turn! Turn!"[1] The phrase *under heaven* is a synonym for *under the sun*.

Under the sun. Sitting in a committee meeting, I wondered when would be an appropriate time to speak up. Some members had strong opinions one way and some the other way. When the chairman asked, "Any other comments?" I raised my hand.

The overall point of the poem is there is an appropriate time for all kinds of human activities, everything done under heaven. Each activity has an opposite which has its own season.

When is the right time to do such and such? Sometimes it is hard to figure out. I live under the sun.

In the Kingdom. My life has had spiritual seasons as well as natural seasons. Sometimes my church was full of life and sometimes it was boring. Sometimes I felt the Holy Spirit every day and sometimes I felt spiritually dry. Sometimes I knew God's righteousness and sometimes I needed to repent.

> We know that all things work together for the good of those who love God, who are called according to his purpose.
>
> Romans 8:28 (CSB)

No matter what the season, God is working in the circumstances of his children, those who love him. Even if seasons seem difficult, he will work them out for their good, because he has good plans for their lives.

Sometimes I received spiritual refreshment, and sometimes I encouraged others. Sometimes I rejoiced in the Lord, and sometimes I repented. The Lord arranges my seasons for my good, so I can fulfill his purposes for me. I live in the Kingdom.

Eternity

Religions all over the world are searching for eternal meaning. Obviously, life is finite, marked by birth and death, but they seek insight into eternity.

Ecclesiastes 3:9–11 (CSB)

---

9 What does the worker gain from his struggles? 10 I have seen the task that God has given the children of Adam to keep them occupied. 11 He has made everything appropriate in its time. He has also put eternity in their hearts, but no one can discover the work God has done from beginning to end.

---

[1] "Turn! Turn! Turn!" (1959) by Pete Seeger, made famous by the music group the Byrds in 1965.

This prose passage expands upon the poem of the previous passage. The end is marked by what God has done. The phrase *children of Adam* means all of humanity.

Under the sun. I can imagine a little kid who thinks his birthday parties are great fun, and so he thinks he should have one every day. He is disappointed to find out birthdays only come once a year, and a year is a long time. Appropriate times for activities is something we learn growing up.

In this passage, the Teacher again paraphrased his quest: What has lasting value? Is it found in any of the activities listed in the above poem? God has ordered creation so everything has an appropriate time, and mankind even has a God-given desire for eternal meaning. However, discovering all of God's created order is beyond human ability.

The natural seasons are obvious to anyone who looks at the weather. However, wisdom can't forecast the weather very well nor discover eternal meaning in life. There are many mysteries in life, like when will my next birthday party happen? I live under the sun.

In the Kingdom. When I lived only under the sun, God's power was obvious in creation. Thunderstorms and lightning were awesome and sunsets were beautiful. I had no excuses.

> What can be known about God is evident among [the pagans], because God has shown it to them. For his invisible attributes, that is, his eternal power and divine nature, have been clearly seen since the creation of the world, being understood through what he has made. As a result, people are without excuse.
>
> Romans 1:19–20 (CSB)

Creation displays God's power and his divine nature. So, people are accountable for their sins.

When I entered the Kingdom, God's involvement in my life was obvious. Sin and righteousness were as different as black and white. He responded to my prayers and worship. Fruits of the Spirit[2] were growing in my life. I live in the Kingdom.

Enjoying life

The key to working a jigsaw puzzle is to see how the pieces fit together. "Where does this one fit?" "Is this an edge piece?" Everyone celebrates when the last piece is put in place. When things are done at the right time, everything fits together.

---

[2] Galatians 5:22–23.

Ecclesiastes 3:12–15 (CSB)

---

12 I know that there is nothing better for them than to rejoice and enjoy the good life. 13 It is also the gift of God whenever anyone eats, drinks, and enjoys all his efforts.

14 I know that everything God does will last forever; there is no adding to it or taking from it. God works so that people will be in awe of him. 15 Whatever is, has already been, and whatever will be, already is. However, God seeks justice for the persecuted.

Like other final passages of major sections, this passage recommends enjoying the good things in life that God provides. The beginning of this passage is marked by the personal action, "I know." The beginning of the second paragraph is also marked by the personal action, "I know," similar to the previous paragraph. The last sentence in the CSB links to the following passage.[3]

Under the sun. God provided my taste buds so I can enjoy birthday cake. My favorite birthday cake used to be German chocolate. However, a friend introduced me to Tiramisu, and now birthdays are even more enjoyable.

The Teacher recommended enjoying the good things God provides. God also provides the ability to enjoy them. In the second paragraph, the Teacher acknowledged that God is eternal and complete. Mankind's response should be worship and righteous living.

Science discovers more complexity in nature every day. God's handiwork is awe inspiring. God had it planned from the beginning, but I just live under the sun.

In the Kingdom. Life under the sun requires my attention most of the day. How can I constantly rejoice, pray, and give thanks when I'm busy with life's necessities?

> Rejoice always, pray constantly, give thanks in everything; for this is God's will for you in Christ Jesus.
>
> 1 Thessalonians 5:16–18 (CSB)

The proper response to God's provision is rejoicing, prayer, and thanksgiving. That is what God wants.

What is my attitude at the moment? Am I smiling? God loves me even when I'm concentrating on a problem. Am I having a mental conversation with God as I go about my day? He is always available and my prayers don't have to be eloquent. Is my attitude thankful for God's provision? I can focus on a task with a thankful attitude.

---

[3]The meaning of the last sentence in 3:15 is uncertain, and thus, translations differ. Shaw, p. 44. Wright, p. 1163. *UBS Old Testament Handbook,* s.v. 3:14–15.

[The faithful] sang the song of God's servant Moses and the song of the Lamb:

> Great and awe-inspiring are your works,
> Lord God, the Almighty;
> just and true are your ways,
> King of the nations.

Revelation 15:3 (CSB)

The faithful in heaven sang a hymn of worship, celebrating the awesome works of God. He is the almighty Creator. His actions are righteous and based on truth. That is why he is the rightful king over all the nations.

My heart joins the faithful in heaven, worshiping the Creator of the universe. Whatever he does is awesome. Worship is not limited to within the walls of a church building. I am free to worship in my heart throughout the day while I'm doing under-the-sun activities. I live in the Kingdom.

8

Evils

When people sin, death is the consequence.

> For the wages of sin is death, but the gift of God is eternal life in
> Christ Jesus our Lord.
>
> Romans 6:23 (CSB)

Death has many forms. Of course, everyone's body eventually dies a natural death. Sin sometimes causes premature death. The Bible speaks of spiritual death, the "second death," on Judgment Day.[1] Suffering and oppression are other forms of death, even though no one's body dies yet. Death affects sin's perpetrators and victims. Creation is often a victim, too, from pollution, ruin, and the unnatural death of plants and animals. Society in general decays. One sin leads to another in cycles of reaction and revenge. It is obvious "the wages of sin is death" under the sun.

God has a solution for sin. Forgiveness is available, because Jesus died on the cross. Death was overcome when Jesus rose from the dead. God's gift of eternal life is a consequence of life in the Kingdom. He cleanses from all unrighteousness.

> Evil people and impostors will become worse, deceiving and being
> deceived. But as for you, continue in what you have learned and
> firmly believed.
>
> 2 Timothy 3:13–14 (CSB)

Sinners are going to sin. Society is being degraded more and more. Deception magnifies the consequences of sin, but like Timothy, citizens of the Kingdom know the truth. The Bible gives us insight into life under the sun and life in the Kingdom.

---

[1] Revelation 20:14–15.

Corruption

If termites infest a house, the structure may fall apart. They do their evil work in hiding. I hired an exterminator to inspect my house each year. I didn't want them to get started. Like termites, sin corrupts society.

Ecclesiastes 3:16–17 (CSB)

---

16 I also observed under the sun: there is wickedness at the place of judgment and there is wickedness at the place of righteousness. 17 I said to myself, "God will judge the righteous and the wicked, since there is a time for every activity and every work."

The beginning of this passage is marked by the personal action, "I also observed under the sun." The end is marked by what God will do.

Under the sun. The local news on TV is often just a list of who the police arrested today. Occasionally a judge or politician is exposed for corruption. Sometimes the audit of a charity finds they spend only a small percentage of their income on good works and the rest goes into salaries of employees.

People sin. Even though we want a righteous legal system, sin corrupts. Even though we expect good motives behind charitable deeds, sin corrupts. God is the righteous judge who will evaluate every person's actions in the end.

Sin happens today just like in the Teacher's time. Irrespective of what human courts do, God's court will hold me accountable for what I do. I live in a world under the sun.

In the Kingdom. I must guard my heart, so it remains soft toward God, rather than stubborn. I must be aware of my heart, so I will repent of selfishness. I can't cling to old sin patterns.

Because of your hardened and unrepentant heart you are storing up wrath for yourself in the day of wrath, when God's righteous judgment is revealed. He will repay each one according to his works: eternal life to those who by persistence in doing good seek glory, honor, and immortality; but wrath and anger to those who are self-seeking and disobey the truth while obeying unrighteousness.

Romans 2:5–8 (CSB)

Those who corrupt justice and refuse to repent of sin will face God's anger. Those who corrupt charitable efforts with selfishness, deception, and unrighteousness will also face God's anger. God will judge each person according to what he has done.

The Bible makes me aware of my own weaknesses. I know God will hold me accountable for my actions, so I will do good instead of sin. I live in the Kingdom.

Mankind and animals

Cognitive scientists and anthropologists can list attributes of *homo sapiens* that make us different from animals, such as language, self-awareness, and making tools. But there is one essential thing we have in common with animals: we all die.

Ecclesiastes 3:18–22 (CSB)

---

18 I said to myself, "This happens so that God may test the children of Adam and they may see for themselves that they are like animals." 19 For the fate of the children of Adam and the fate of animals is the same. As one dies, so dies the other; they all have the same breath. People have no advantage over animals since everything is futile.

20 All are going to the same place; all come from dust, and all return to dust. 21 Who knows if the spirits of the children of Adam go upward and the spirits of animals go downward to the earth?

22 I have seen that there is nothing better than for a person to enjoy his activities because that is his reward. For who can enable him to see what will happen after he dies?

The beginning of this passage is marked by the personal action, "I said to myself." The end of this passage recommends enjoying the activities of life. The phrase *children of Adam* means all of humanity.

Under the sun. I mourn when a family member dies. I mourn when a family pet dies, too. Both breathed the same air. Whether buried or cremated, their bodies return to dust. I no longer have the friendship of their touch. That is why I should enjoy family and pets today. After death will be too late.

Death is the consequence of sin. In this passage, the Teacher compared deaths of people to deaths of animals. They are similar. People and land animals both breathe the air. Their dead bodies decompose. We can't see what happens after death for humans or animals. This similarity means everything is vanity. So, the Teacher recommended enjoying one's activities while still alive.

I will enjoy the companionship of friends, family, and pets while I live under the sun.

In the Kingdom. I don't have as many hairs as I used to. I wonder if God assigned an angel to keep track of them. I must be keeping him busy.

Aren't two sparrows sold for a penny? Yet not one of them falls to the ground without your Father's consent. But even the hairs of your head have all been counted. So don't be afraid; you are worth more than many sparrows.

Matthew 10:29–31 (CSB)

The Teacher thought people and animals are similar, because both die. God values people much more than animals. God is attentive to the fate of a sparrow, but people are worth more than many sparrows. People are so valuable to God, he keeps track of small things like the number of hairs on my head.

It is comforting to know the heavenly Father cares about all my details. I know he is interested when I pray about any little thing. I live in the Kingdom.

Oppression

In a collegiate wrestling competition, the goal is to control one's opponent. The match can be won by pinning the opponent's shoulders or shoulder blades to the mat for at least a second. Likewise, when criminals or the government oppresses people, the goal is control.

Ecclesiastes 4:1–3 (CSB)

---

1 Again, I observed all the acts of oppression being done under the sun. Look at the tears of those who are oppressed; they have no one to comfort them. Power is with those who oppress them; they have no one to comfort them.

2 So I commended the dead, who have already died, more than the living, who are still alive. 3 But better than either of them is the one who has not yet existed, who has not seen the evil activity that is done under the sun.

The beginning of this passage is marked by the personal action, "Again, I observed." The phrase *under the sun* brackets the beginning and the end of the passage.

Under the sun. There have been times when I was cheated and had no recourse. I just had to accept the loss and go on with life. I felt oppressed.

Throughout human history, the strong have sinned by oppressing the weak. Victims usually are helpless and have no one to comfort them. The Teacher compared the victims to the dead and to an unborn child. The dead are no longer suffering oppression, but the unborn child is even better off, because he has not yet seen any oppression.

When I die, those times I was cheated won't matter. They won't matter to future generations either. I may be cheated again sometime, because I live under the sun.

In the Kingdom. I had to forgive those who cheated me. That decision freed me from feeling oppressed. The Lord provided for me later, so I didn't miss what was taken from me.

> [Jesus] came to Nazareth, where he had been brought up. As usual, he entered the synagogue on the Sabbath day and stood up to read. The scroll of the prophet Isaiah was given to him, and unrolling the scroll, he found the place where it was written:
>
> > The Spirit of the Lord is on me,
> > because he has anointed me ...
> > to set free the oppressed,
> > to proclaim the year of the Lord's favor.
>
> He then rolled up the scroll, gave it back to the attendant, and sat down. And the eyes of everyone in the synagogue were fixed on him. He began by saying to them, "Today as you listen, this Scripture has been fulfilled."
>
> Luke 4:16–21 (CSB)

Part of Jesus' purpose was to set free the oppressed. Life in the Kingdom is free from oppression, because Jesus has defeated sin. Even though oppression under the sun may still happen, it has lost its power to intimidate. Oppression will be swept away when Jesus returns and all sin is judged.

My sins are forgiven. I am free from them in my soul. I may be a victim of someone's sin, but I know about God's power and provision on my behalf. So loss of material things doesn't matter. I live in the Kingdom.

Jealousy

I wanted to do an excellent job. I carefully analyzed the task at hand. I put forth my best effort. Did I succeed? What was my motivation?

Ecclesiastes 4:4–6 (CSB)

---

4 I saw that all labor and all skillful work is due to one person's jealousy of another. This too is futile and a pursuit of the wind.

> 5 The fool folds his arms
> and consumes his own flesh.
> 6 Better one handful with rest
> than two handfuls with effort and a pursuit of the wind.

The beginning of this passage is marked by the personal action, "I saw." The end of the prose is marked by declaring this too is vanity and chasing the wind, followed by a pair of proverbs.

Under the sun. Becky learned to play chess when she was five years old. When she lost playing Uncle Eddie, she threw a tantrum. She wasn't ready to respond to competition in a positive way.

One of the Ten Commandments is "Thou shalt not covet."[2] The sins of jealousy and pride motivate people to compete in many areas of life. The Teacher concluded this also is vanity and chasing the wind. The first proverb teaches that a fool's idleness is not the answer to jealousy. The second proverb recommends being satisfied instead of striving for more.

I received advertisements in the mail from three home-improvement companies which all promised to do the best job. They were motivated to work hard. They were competing for my business. Competition is normal in modern society. I live under the sun.

In the Kingdom. When I was in high school, I played table tennis against my Dad every evening. The desire to win was a motivator, but I learned that winning or losing were not important in our relationship.

> For where there is envy and selfish ambition, there is disorder and every evil practice.
>
> James 3:16 (CSB)

The New Testament teaches that envy and selfish ambition are sin, namely, jealousy. This sin in attitude results in chaos and evil actions. Skillful competitive accomplishments do not redeem wrong motives.

Envy and selfish ambition have no place in the Kingdom. That means I must honor others, even those who beat me in a sport. I live in the Kingdom.

Loneliness

Every Boy Scout knows whenever you go swimming, you should have a buddy. This is especially important when you swim in the ocean. Sharks sometimes look for dinner in the surf. Your buddy might see one coming.

Ecclesiastes 4:7–12 (CSB)

---

7 Again, I saw futility under the sun: 8 There is a person without a companion, without even a son or brother, and though there is no end to all his struggles, his eyes are still not content with riches. "Who am I struggling for," he asks, "and depriving myself of good things?" This too is futile and a miserable task.

9 Two are better than one because they have a good reward for their efforts. 10 For if either falls, his companion can lift him up; but pity the one who falls without another to lift him up. 11 Also, if two lie down together, they can keep warm; but how can one person

---

[2]Exodus 20:17 (KJV).

alone keep warm? 12 And if someone overpowers one person, two can resist him. A cord of three strands is not easily broken.

The beginning of this passage is marked by the personal action, "Again, I saw futility under the sun." The first paragraph ends declaring this too is vanity. The second paragraph is a series of illustrations. The last sentence of the passage is a metaphor that summarizes the passage.

Under the sun. I felt isolated when I started a new job near a big city. My relatives are scattered across the country. It was difficult to build and maintain family relationships when separated by such distances. I wrote letters often. Relationships are important to me.

Sometimes circumstances leave a person alone. The Teacher did not say why this situation occurred. Loneliness is a product of society's dysfunction. Life becomes a struggle, and even if one works hard to become wealthy, the result is vanity. Perhaps he is a workaholic. When one has a partner, they work with each other, lift up each other, and protect each other. When exposed to the weather, they can warm each other. Healthy relationships are essential.

Modern society seems to separate and isolate people. Families too often become fractured by sin. It takes effort to build relationships, especially when there is no family nearby. Modern technology may make reaching out easier than letter writing, but it still takes effort. I live under the sun.

In the Kingdom. When I was single, I shared a house with three other guys from my church. We had dinner together once a week. We shared chores including grocery shopping. A prospective housemate was surprised we trusted each other enough to have a common checkbook for groceries and other expenses; he decided not to join us. Love for one another gets expressed in many ways.

> I give you a new command: Love one another. Just as I have loved you, you are also to love one another. By this everyone will know that you are my disciples, if you love one another.
>
> John 13:34–35 (CSB)

Life under the sun doesn't guarantee a companion; sometimes one is alone. Jesus' new command is to love other disciples in the same way Jesus loves us. Life in the Kingdom is life in community with other Christians.

Whenever I moved to a new place, I sought out a church home where the people loved one another. I have had to build family-like relationships with local Christians. It takes time and effort. Some people are more open than others. I treasure all those relationships. I live in the Kingdom.

Royal succession

Sometimes there is a change of party when there is an election. The handover of power is supposed to be smooth, but it's not always friendly.

Ecclesiastes 4:13–16 (CSB)

---

13 Better is a poor but wise youth than an old but foolish king who no longer pays attention to warnings. 14 For he came from prison to be king, even though he was born poor in his kingdom. 15 I saw all the living, who move about under the sun, follow a second youth who succeeds him. 16 There is no limit to all the people who were before them, yet those who come later will not rejoice in him. This too is futile and a pursuit of the wind.

The passage begins with a "better than" clause. The end of the passage is marked by declaring this too is vanity and chasing the wind.

Under the sun. Businesses sometimes have "palace intrigue." A guy I worked with, who was denied the project manager job, started his own consulting firm and persuaded the client of his old job to make him effective project manager.

This passage illustrates the intrigue of royal succession with a story having three characters: A first youth, an old king, and a second youth. The first youth supplanted the old king, because he was wise and the old king was foolish. The second youth supplanted the first youth, because he had a following among the people. This cycle is repeated throughout history, yet no one in following generations respected their memory. The Teacher concluded it is vanity and chasing the wind.

Even though I've never worked for royalty, I've seen businesses face leadership succession. The dynamics are similar for the person at the top or just a working supervisor. Palace intrigue happens at all levels. I live under the sun.

In the Kingdom. My wife and I were assigned to watch over several home Bible studies for a time. Some groups did well and some had problems. We did whatever we could to help the leaders of those groups. Leadership in a local church is hard.

Jesus called [the disciples] over and said, "You know that the rulers of the Gentiles lord it over them, and those in high positions act as tyrants over them. It must not be like that among you. On the contrary, whoever wants to become great among you must be your servant, and whoever wants to be first among you must be your slave; just as the Son of Man did not come to be served, but to serve, and to give his life as a ransom for many."

Matthew 20:25–28 (CSB)

Palace intrigue is motivated by lust for power. High positions reinforce selfish pride. Jesus told his disciples the Kingdom is not like that. Those who want to be great in the Kingdom must behave as a servant like Jesus did. A high sounding office with power over others is not the goal.

After reading these verses in Matthew, it sounds like an official position in an institutional church is a spiritual trap; I don't want to be a tyrant. I appreciate the humble leadership of others at my local churches. They have been godly examples for me. I live in the Kingdom.

Hasty vows to God

I went to the car dealer to buy a new car. I had a certain price in mind. The sales manager had other ideas. We had to negotiate. Some people go to church to negotiate with God.

Ecclesiastes 5:1–7 (CSB)

---

1 Guard your steps when you go to the house of God. Better to approach in obedience than to offer the sacrifice as fools do, for they ignorantly do wrong. 2 Do not be hasty to speak, and do not be impulsive to make a speech before God. God is in heaven and you are on earth, so let your words be few. 3 Just as dreams accompany much labor, so also a fool's voice comes with many words. 4 When you make a vow to God, don't delay fulfilling it, because he does not delight in fools. Fulfill what you vow. 5 Better that you do not vow than that you vow and not fulfill it. 6 Do not let your mouth bring guilt on you, and do not say in the presence of the messenger that it was a mistake. Why should God be angry with your words and destroy the work of your hands? 7 For many dreams bring futility; so do many words. Therefore, fear God.

This passage consists of warnings about hasty vows to God. The end is marked by declaring many dreams bring vanity, followed by a summary warning, "Therefore, fear God."

Under the sun. When my church was raising money for the building fund, I was shocked when someone pledged to give a huge amount. Not long afterward, the donor was offended by something the pastor said and left the church. The big gift never materialized.

The Teacher assumed everyone would go to the temple for usual religious duties, such as sacrifices. Apparently, some people didn't do things properly. He warned not to make foolish speeches to God on spur of the moment. Some people make long winded vows to God and then forget about it. God expects one to fulfill his vows. Failing to fulfill a vow is sin; it is lying to God. It is better to not vow at all. Hasty vows are vanity. Fearing God, on the other hand, will guard one's mouth.

When I'm around religious people, it is tempting to act religious. Eloquent prayers and big contributions are what they expect. Whenever my church is raising money for a project, common sense says it is better to just write a check for my contribution, rather than pledge a future offering. I live under the sun.

In the Kingdom. As I was reading the "love chapter" in my devotional time, I saw that love in action means being kind.[3] I resolved to be kind instead of cynical and sarcastic. I didn't need to explain it to God. I didn't need to swear that I was sincere. He already knew my heart.

> Above all, my brothers and sisters, do not swear, either by heaven or by earth or with any other oath. But let your "yes" mean "yes," and your "no" mean "no," so that you won't fall under judgment.
>
> James 5:12 (CSB)

Jesus taught his disciples not to make oaths,[4] and James summarized what Jesus had said. Oaths are not necessary to validate what I say or to say something emphatically.

The Teacher saw fools making promises to God. Some people will make a vow to God to try to impress him or to negotiate with him. The heavenly Father is not interested in my vow, because he is already giving me good things.

I am determined to always tell the truth, so oaths and vows will not be necessary. I live in the Kingdom.

Perversion of justice

Lord Acton[5] is famous for his remark, "Power tends to corrupt. Absolute power corrupts absolutely."

Ecclesiastes 5:8–9 (CSB)

---

8 If you see oppression of the poor and perversion of justice and righteousness in the province, don't be astonished at the situation, because one official protects another official, and higher officials protect them. 9 The profit from the land is taken by all; the king is served by the field.

This passage explains how perversions of justice occur.[6]

---

[3] 1 Corinthians 13:4.
[4] Matthew 5:33–37.
[5] John Dalberg-Acton, First Baron Acton (1834–1902) of England.
[6] The meaning of this passage is uncertain. *UBS Old Testament Handbook, s.v.* 5:8.

Under the sun. When I worked for government contractors, I saw unethical business practices by companies and colluding government officials. Higher level officials would often cover up the sins of lower level officials instead of correcting abuses. Sometimes government officials were rewarded with lucrative jobs with corrupt companies.

The Teacher saw that sin among government officials resulted in oppression, twisting of justice, and unrighteousness. Officials protected each other so that they all got rich, exploiting the people, and even the king got his share.

Perversion of justice is obvious. Just a little honest investigation is needed. The average person is helpless to enforce correction. It's frustrating. I live under the sun.

In the Kingdom. There are consequences when corruption perverts justice. In one company, there were seven layers of management above me. Within about three years, six of the seven had either been fired, demoted, or retired under duress.

> The eyes of the Lord are on the righteous
> and his ears are open to their prayer.
> But the face of the Lord is against
> those who do what is evil.
>
> 1 Peter 3:12 (CSB)

God knows all about perversions of justice and what corrupt government officials do. They can't hide their sins from him. He responds to the prayers of those in the Kingdom, and he will judge evildoers.

When I saw perversions of justice by those in management above me, I could only pray to the Lord for righteousness to prevail. I live in the Kingdom.

Loving wealth

In 2009, the Florida Lottery awarded its first Powerball jackpot, The winner elected to take home over one hundred million dollars cash. Millions of people play the lottery hoping to get rich.

Ecclesiastes 5:10–12 (CSB)

---

10 The one who loves silver is never satisfied with silver, and whoever loves wealth is never satisfied with income. This too is futile.

11 When good things increase, the ones who consume them multiply; what, then, is the profit to the owner, except to gaze at them with his eyes?

12 The sleep of the worker is sweet, whether he eats little or much, but the abundance of the rich permits him no sleep.

The perversion of justice in the previous passage was motivated by the sin of greed. This passage consists of three related proverbs mixed with comments.

Under the sun. Some of my friends became involved in a pyramid marketing scheme. They thought they could get rich quick without much effort. Before long, the scheme collapsed. Hardly anybody wanted to buy the product.

Greed is sin. The first proverb points out that greed is never satisfied. There is never enough. The Teacher concluded this too is vanity.

The second proverb says when one does become rich, those who want handouts multiply. The Teacher concluded that riches don't have any lasting benefit to the owner.

Relatives of an athlete on my college campus thought he would make the rest of the family rich. They pressured him to go professional before finishing school and ruined his prospects.

The third proverb contrasts the sleep of a worker and a rich man. The worker has real rest, but the rich man worries about his wealth all night.

A friend worked as a day-trader in the stock market for his own account. He bought and sold stocks and other securities at a frantic pace. The stress became too much, so he switched careers to teaching day-trading instead of doing it.

When I see these proverbs fulfilled in the lives of my friends and acquaintances, it's obvious I live under the sun.

In the Kingdom. If you ask someone, "Do you want to be rich?" almost everyone will say "Yes!" even those who are Christians.

> But those who want to be rich fall into temptation, a trap, and many foolish and harmful desires, which plunge people into ruin and destruction. For the love of money is a root of all kinds of evil, and by craving it, some have wandered away from the faith and pierced themselves with many griefs.
>
> 1 Timothy 6:9–10 (CSB)

Chapter 6 of this letter to Timothy has an extended discussion about money and greed which is relevant to several passages in Ecclesiastes. This is the first installment.

Wanting to be rich is the first step toward ruin and grief. The Teacher said the love of money is never satisfied. Paul told Timothy the love of money leads to abandoning the faith and many evils.

I was surprised to see in these verses it is foolish to want to become rich. I realized I had the responsibility before God to use whatever he gave me in a godly way, so I searched the Scriptures to find out what that means.[7] I live in the Kingdom.

---

[7]Edward B. Allen, *Love, Sex, Money, and Power: A Devotional Commentary* (Melbourne, Florida: Edward B. Allen, 2017).

Struggling empty–handed

A manufacturing company was started by seven partners. After a number of successful years, the company was bought by another company with the understanding that the original management team would continue to run the subsidiary. However, after a short time, the parent company closed the plant. No employees transferred, and the business disappeared.

Ecclesiastes 5:13–17 (CSB)

---

13 There is a sickening tragedy I have seen under the sun: wealth kept by its owner to his harm. 14 That wealth was lost in a bad venture, so when he fathered a son, he was empty-handed.

15 As he came from his mother's womb, so he will go again, naked as he came; he will take nothing for his efforts that he can carry in his hands. 16 This too is a sickening tragedy: exactly as he comes, so he will go. What does the one gain who struggles for the wind? 17 What is more, he eats in darkness all his days, with much frustration, sickness, and anger.

The beginning of this passage is marked by the personal action, "There is a sickening tragedy I have seen under the sun." The ending declares "frustration, sickness, and anger." The words *sickening* and *sickness* bracket the beginning and end of the passage.

Under the sun. A friend started a shop selling donuts and ice cream. He was counting on God to make his business successful. However, he made some poor business decisions and the shop failed. He then became bitter.

The Teacher saw wealth was easily lost in a failed business venture. When that man died, he had nothing to pass on as an inheritance, and he could not take anything with him.[8] His struggles gaining and losing wealth were like chasing the wind.

Greed produces frustration, sickness, and anger when hopes are destroyed. Business ventures are always risky under the sun.

In the Kingdom. I was given a set of yearbooks from my college covering 1896 through 1908. I enjoyed looking at them, but after many years, I had to let go of them. So, I shipped them to the school's library.

For we brought nothing into the world, and we can take nothing out. If we have food and clothing, we will be content with these.
1 Timothy 6:7–8 (CSB)

---

[8]In this passage, it is ambiguous whether the pronoun *he* refers to the father or the child. The CSB reads as the father. *UBS Old Testament Handbook, s.v.* 5:14 prefers the child.

Paul agreed with the Teacher: one cannot take anything with him when he dies. Therefore, we should be content with basic necessities, rather than chasing wealth.

Accumulating stuff is not the road to contentment. I know I have more than basic necessities. Much of my extra stuff is actually a distraction from the Kingdom. It is taking persistent work to simplify my life. I live in the Kingdom.

Enjoying life

Evil is so pervasive in this world that all seem to be vanity. There are countless victims of sin. However, one can still find moments to enjoy good things God provides.

Ecclesiastes 5:18–20 (CSB)

18 Here is what I have seen to be good: It is appropriate to eat, drink, and experience good in all the labor one does under the sun during the few days of his life God has given him, because that is his reward.

19 Furthermore, everyone to whom God has given riches and wealth, he has also allowed him to enjoy them, take his reward, and rejoice in his labor. This is a gift of God, 20 for he does not often consider the days of his life because God keeps him occupied with the joy of his heart.

The beginning of this passage is marked by the personal action, "Here is what I have seen to be good." The end is marked by the good God has done.

Under the sun. Each winter, the roads in Florida become crowded with cars from out of state. The snowbirds are mostly retired and are rich enough to escape the snow and spend several months each year in Florida. Many of the condominium apartments near the beach are occupied only in the winter. Golf courses become busy. The snowbirds enjoy the warm weather.

This passage concludes this major section by recommending that one enjoy God's provision in spite of all the sin under the sun. In spite of a limited lifespan, God gives one the ability to enjoy the fruits of his work.

My short lifespan is a gift from God. The ability to enjoy daily life is also a gift from God. Even though the summers are hot, I enjoy the warm winter weather like the snowbirds. I live under the Florida sun.

In the Kingdom. My wife had a piano. Both of us were more interested in playing guitar than piano, so we gave the piano to a friend who used it daily.

> Instruct those who are rich in the present age not to be arrogant or to set their hope on the uncertainty of wealth, but on God, who richly provides us with all things to enjoy. Instruct them to do what is good, to be rich in good works, to be generous and willing to share, storing up treasure for themselves as a good foundation for the coming age, so that they may take hold of what is truly life.
>
> 1 Timothy 6:17–19 (CSB)

How should the wealthy live in the Kingdom? A rich believer should live with humility, knowing wealth is only temporary and can easily be lost. Like the Teacher, Paul recommended enjoying what God gives. A rich believer has resources for good works, generosity, and sharing, resulting in treasure in heaven. Living generously in the Kingdom is true life.

Any citizen of the Kingdom can develop a generous lifestyle. When I have an item I don't need, I ask myself, "Who would benefit from using it?" When I give something away, I feel like an investor in the Kingdom. I live in the Kingdom.

9

Life without contentment

Modern society is bombarded with advertisements trying to create demand for more, more, and more. Advertising is designed to make one unhappy with the current situation. They seem to say, "If you will only buy my product, your life will be so much better."

Riches without enjoyment

I saw the play *Rosencratz and Guildenstern are Dead* at a theater. The lead characters of this play are minor characters from Shakespeare's tragedy *Hamlet*. The play presented tragic elements of existential philosophy. Similar to Shakespeare's play, it is announced at the end, "Rosencratz and Guildenstern are dead." Tragedies in art often mirror tragedies in life.

Ecclesiastes 6:1–2 (CSB)

---

1 Here is a tragedy I have observed under the sun, and it weighs heavily on humanity: 2 God gives a person riches, wealth, and honor so that he lacks nothing of all he desires for himself, but God does not allow him to enjoy them. Instead, a stranger will enjoy them. This is futile and a sickening tragedy.

The beginning of this passage is marked by the personal action, "Here is a tragedy I have observed under the sun." The end is marked by declaring this is vanity. Also, the word *tragedy* brackets the passage.

Under the sun. Brad was a successful professor in his field. At the peak of his career, he died of cancer. All who knew him considered his death a tragedy.

The Teacher was depressed by what he saw. Sometimes a person acquires wealth and fame, but can't enjoy them. Perhaps he dies prematurely. Perhaps he loses the wealth in a business venture. Perhaps addiction or personal tragedy intervene. Honor evaporates, and a stranger gets to enjoy the wealth. Such a situation is yet another example of vanity.

When I read about such tragedies or if I know the victim personally, my heart aches. I live under the sun.

In the Kingdom. A friend gave me directions to a home Bible study. There was a guard at the gate of the neighborhood. When I got to the house, I could see it was very expensive. About thirty people gathered in the living room. Food for everyone was set out in another room. This host was using what God had given him for building the Kingdom.

> Then [Jesus] told [the crowd] a parable: A rich man's land was very productive. He thought to himself, 'What should I do, since I don't have anywhere to store my crops? I will do this,' he said. 'I'll tear down my barns and build bigger ones and store all my grain and my goods there. Then I'll say to myself, "You have many goods stored up for many years. Take it easy; eat, drink, and enjoy yourself." '
>
> But God said to him, 'You fool! This very night your life is demanded of you. And the things you have prepared—whose will they be?'
>
> That's how it is with the one who stores up treasure for himself and is not rich toward God.
>
> Luke 12:16–21 (CSB)

Jesus told a parable of a successful man who needed more room to store his wealth. As he planned a construction project, he did not know he would die that night. Jesus agreed with the Teacher. It is a tragedy when someone accumulates wealth but can't enjoy it. The better alternative is to accumulate treasure in heaven through a rich relationship with God.

I tend to save stuff "just in case I need it later." "I need bigger boxes to store my stuff." Hoarding is a symptom of a selfish attitude. I have to repent when I see myself selfishly saving instead of being generous, because I live in the Kingdom.

Long life without satisfaction

"I Can't Get No Satisfaction" is a song by the rock band the Rolling Stones.[1] The lyrics convey a cynical frustrated reaction to life.

Ecclesiastes 6:3–7 (CSB)

---

3 A man may father a hundred children and live many years. No matter how long he lives, if he is not satisfied by good things and

---

[1] "I Can't Get No Satisfaction" (1965) by Mick Jagger and Keith Richards.

does not even have a proper burial, I say that a stillborn child is better off than he. 4 For he comes in futility and he goes in darkness, and his name is shrouded in darkness. 5 Though a stillborn child does not see the sun and is not conscious, it has more rest than he. 6 And if a person lives a thousand years twice, but does not experience happiness, do not both go to the same place?

> 7 All of a person's labor is for his stomach,
> yet the appetite is never satisfied.

This passage consists of an illustration of someone who lived many years, but never found satisfaction.[2] The end of this passage is marked by a proverb. This passage uses exaggeration for emphasis.

Under the sun. I can imagine a man who was a workaholic. He was so dedicated to his job he hardly had time for his wife and kids. When the kids were grown she divorced him. In his old age, he died alone.

Most people want to raise children and to live a long life. The man the Teacher described had all these, but was never satisfied enough to enjoy them. The Teacher concluded a still-born child has more rest than this man, and besides, death comes to both of them. The proverb at the end points out that selfish desires are never satisfied.

Finding satisfaction in life is more important than achieving a comfortable lifestyle. Long life is wasted if one does not experience fulfilling relationships under the sun.

In the Kingdom. Self-help books advise job applicants to negotiate for a good salary. They assume one must strive to become wealthy, and that will in turn result in a satisfying lifestyle.

> Keep your life free from the love of money. Be satisfied with what you have, for he himself has said, "I will never leave you or abandon you."
>
> Hebrews 13:5 (CSB)

Refusing to love money is the first step toward contentment. A believer can be satisfied with whatever he has, because God is always nearby to provide as needs arise.

Throughout my career, I never had to negotiate for a big salary. Sometimes I was given a bigger salary than I expected; sometimes I got raises; and sometimes God arranged for lower expenses in life. God provided what I needed. I live in the Kingdom.

---

[2] Bible scholars debate the meaning of *no proper burial*. Shaw, p. 81.

Wisdom without advantage

When race cars line up for the start, the pole position has the advantage of being in front on the inside of the track. People look for an advantage in life, too.

Ecclesiastes 6:8–12 (CSB)

---

8 What advantage then does the wise person have over the fool? What advantage is there for the poor person who knows how to conduct himself before others? 9 Better what the eyes see than wandering desire. This too is futile and a pursuit of the wind.

10 Whatever exists was given its name long ago, and it is known what mankind is. But he is not able to contend with the one stronger than he. 11 For when there are many words, they increase futility.

What is the advantage for mankind? 12 For who knows what is good for anyone in life, in the few days of his futile life that he spends like a shadow? Who can tell anyone what will happen after him under the sun?

The first and last paragraphs of this passage ask the question, "What is the advantage?" The first and second paragraphs end with a declaration of vanity. The third paragraph mentions "his futile life" which is similar. So, these paragraphs are grouped into the same passage.

Under the sun. Many people aspire to live their dream lifestyle: a big house, beautifully landscaped, and a boat ready to go, parked in the driveway. However, the wife got tired of cleaning the big house. The flower beds grew weeds faster than they grew flowers. You may have heard about boats: "A boat is a hole in the water you pour money into," or "The best two days in a man's life are the day he buys a boat and the day he sells it." Maybe the dream lifestyle is not all it seems.

The first paragraph of this passage asks whether wisdom is worthwhile, even if one is poor. The proverb indicates being satisfied is better than many desires. The Teacher concluded such desires are vanity and like chasing the wind.

The second paragraph explains that God has planned his creation from the beginning and long arguments with God are vanity.

The third paragraph asks whether there is any lasting value for mankind. Does anyone know what a good life consists of? The implied answer is no one, and the future is completely out of a person's control.

Only God knows my future and what a good life consists of for me. Even if I am wise, arguing with God over human desires is just vanity. I live under the sun.

In the Kingdom. I became a Christian believer as a boy, so my personal development and my spiritual development gradually grew in parallel.

> But godliness with contentment is great gain.
>
> 1 Timothy 6:6 (CSB)

In the world, people measure advantage in dollars and cents. In the Kingdom, profit is found in godliness and contentment.

Personal maturity grows with experience under the sun. Spiritual maturity grows with experience in the Kingdom. Godliness develops as a believer's character is molded by the Holy Spirit. Contentment develops as one experiences God's loving care. I live in the Kingdom.

10

Characteristics of the wise

Becoming a wise person is obviously better than being a fool. Applying wisdom to my life seems complicated, because I face so many different situations. This section discusses characteristics of the wise and gives advice for wise living.

Mourning

Mourning is how I express the grief I feel when a loved one dies. Death is a natural part of life. Reflecting on the lives of loved ones forces me to be serious about my own life.

Ecclesiastes 7:1–6 (CSB)

---

1 A good name is better than fine perfume,
and the day of one's death is better than the day of one's birth.
2 It is better to go to a house of mourning
than to go to a house of feasting,
since that is the end of all mankind,
and the living should take it to heart.
3 Grief is better than laughter,
for when a face is sad, a heart may be glad.
4 The heart of the wise is in a house of mourning,
but the heart of fools is in a house of pleasure.
5 It is better to listen to rebuke from a wise person
than to listen to the song of fools,
6 for like the crackling of burning thorns under the pot,
so is the laughter of the fool.
This too is futile.

This passage consists of a series of proverbs related to death and mourning. The passage ends declaring this too is vanity.

Under the sun. I attended the funeral of a friend's adult son who was killed in a motorcycle accident. His friends and family shared about their precious times together.

The Teacher thought a good reputation is nice to have, but at birth one will face so much vanity ahead that relief at death is better. Death is the time for mourning. The wise prefer funerals to parties. Fools prefer superficial pleasures, laughter, and singing, but the wise reflect on life and death. The last proverb is an analogy between thorns quickly burning in a kitchen fire and the laughter of fools. The Teacher concluded that the attitude of fools is vanity.

Funerals make me reflect on life and how easily dangerous thrills can end it. I live under the sun.

In the Kingdom. A funeral for an atheist is a sad occasion, because the deceased had no hope for life after death. Funerals for believers have both grief over the loss of companionship and rejoicing over hope for resurrection and eternal life. Jesus' resurrection demonstrated his victory over sin and death.

> The trumpet will sound, and the dead will be raised incorruptible, and we will be changed. For this corruptible body must be clothed with incorruptibility, and this mortal body must be clothed with immortality. When this corruptible body is clothed with incorruptibility, and this mortal body is clothed with immortality, then the saying that is written will take place:
>
> > Death has been swallowed up in victory.
> > Where, death, is your victory?
> > Where, death, is your sting?
>
> The sting of death is sin, and the power of sin is the law. But thanks be to God, who gives us the victory through our Lord Jesus Christ!
>
> 1 Corinthians 15:52–57 (CSB)

The Teacher couldn't see beyond death. The New Testament acknowledges that all die, but believers have hope because Jesus rose from the dead. When Jesus returns, the dead in Christ will be resurrected to immortal bodies. Sin and death will finally be defeated. I live in the Kingdom.

Avoiding a corrupt mind

A wise person will reject anything that would corrupt his mind. Many will entice one with evil schemes that cloud one's judgment. Even a wise person will be tempted.

Ecclesiastes 7:7 (CSB)

---

7 Surely, the practice of extortion turns a wise person into a fool,
and a bribe corrupts the mind.

This brief passage is a proverb.

Under the sun. A businessman who is confronted with extortion cannot make wise business decisions. If he resists extortion, the criminals may destroy his business. If he yields to extortion, he will have to pay the criminals.

Corruption, such as extortion or bribery, will ruin a person's life, even a wise person's life. The proverb doesn't say whether the person is a victim or perpetrator. The result is bad either way, so anyone who wants to maintain his wisdom will avoid such corruption.

Sometimes a government official is offered a "business opportunity" that is too good to be true. When he takes a bribe, he cannot render impartial justice. When someone offers a bribe, he, too, has lost his moral compass. Extortion and bribery happen under the sun.

In the Kingdom. When I had resigned from my job, my department manager conducted an exit interview. I explained how I could not participate in an unethical business practice. He understood the issue but said he was too far along in his career to take a stand. I was sad for him.

> But each person is tempted when he is drawn away and enticed by his own evil desire. Then after desire has conceived, it gives birth to sin, and when sin is fully grown, it gives birth to death.
>
> James 1:14–15 (CSB)

A corrupt mind is the result of sin. James explained sin's progression: temptation, selfish desires, sin in action, and eventually, death.

Living in the Kingdom gives me a clear understanding of how sin destroys. This helps me to recognize temptation promptly and to resist its appeal. I don't always reject temptation, but I'm thankful God's forgiveness is available when I repent. I live in the Kingdom.

Patience

"Patience" from the album *Music Machine*[1] is one of my favorite songs. The song tells the story of Herbert the snail who has to learn to "have patience." Sometimes I have to sing it to myself.

---

[1] "Patience" on the album *Music Machine: The Fruit of the Spirit* by Candle (1977).

Ecclesiastes 7:8–10 (CSB)

---

8 The end of a matter is better than its beginning;
a patient spirit is better than a proud spirit.
9 Don't let your spirit rush to be angry,
for anger abides in the heart of fools.
10 Don't say, "Why were the former days better than these?"
since it is not wise of you to ask this.

This passage is a series of three proverbs. The first proverb commends patience directly. The following proverbs elaborate.

Under the sun. Modern life values instant gratification instead of patience. Microwave ovens are popular because they can cook dinner in minutes. I'd rather not wait hours while dinner simmers on the stove.

Each of the Teacher's proverbs gives a practical lesson. Patiently waiting for a matter to play out is the strategy of the wise. A proud person will rush to get involved. The quick-tempered person is a fool. Nostalgia is motivated by dissatisfaction with one's current situation. It is easy to blame God for the evils of the present day.

When the news media report some outrageous event, an army of people instantly express their opinions on social media. Some might ask, "Why doesn't God do something about this terrible situation?" Then later, one learns more about what happened. The true story wasn't as it appeared, and the supposed victim was not so innocent after all. It is wise to wait for the facts to come out before reacting. I live under the sun.

In the Kingdom. My wife tells me I speculate too much. For example, while driving down the road, I saw an empty building and proceeded to guess why it was empty and what will go in there next—speculate, speculate.

> My dear brothers and sisters, understand this: Everyone should be quick to listen, slow to speak, and slow to anger, for human anger does not accomplish God's righteousness.
>
> James 1:19–20 (CSB)

Patience is a godly virtue, a fruit of the Holy Spirit. Listening to others instead of offering instant opinions yields understanding. Anger leads to sin. So patiently waiting for a situation to unfold is the best course.

I should be patient before I spout my opinions. I must repent when I refuse to listen and get angry. I live in the Kingdom.

Handling adversity

The stress is unbearable. Your nerves are on edge. Your stomach is in knots. You can't think about anything else... Everyone faces adversity from time to time. Responding with wisdom helps one come through a bad situation.

Ecclesiastes 7:11–14 (CSB)

---

11 Wisdom is as good as an inheritance
and an advantage to those who see the sun,
12 because wisdom is protection as silver is protection;
but the advantage of knowledge
is that wisdom preserves the life of its owner.
13 Consider the work of God,
for who can straighten out
what he has made crooked?

14 In the day of prosperity be joyful, but in the day of adversity, consider: God has made the one as well as the other, so that no one can discover anything that will come after him.

This passage begins with poetry about wisdom and concludes with a prose recommendation. The end is marked by what God has done.

Under the sun. The stress on my job gave me stomach pain. Common sense told me the aggravations at work were just temporary. I had to adjust my attitude.

Wisdom is helpful in life. Wisdom may even save a person's life. But life under the sun is temporary. God's work is permanent. The Teacher advised one to rejoice when life goes well and to be thoughtful in adversity. Both seasons are part of God's creation.

Like everyone, I've had seasons of adversity. When I adjusted my attitude with common sense, my stomach felt much better. I live under the sun.

In the Kingdom. Persecution of Christians is rampant in some places. For example, churches are closed and pastors are imprisoned in China. Christians are falsely accused of insulting the Prophet in Pakistan. Terrorists burn Christian villages and kidnap Christian girls in Nigeria.

> But you have followed my teaching, conduct, purpose, faith, patience, love, and endurance, along with the persecutions and sufferings that came to me in Antioch, Iconium, and Lystra. What persecutions I endured—and yet the Lord rescued me from them all. In fact, all who want to live a godly life in Christ Jesus will be persecuted.
>
> 2 Timothy 3:10–12 (CSB)

63

The day of adversity is a normal part of life under the sun. A Christian should also expect persecution and perhaps death as a martyr, because the world is opposed to God's purposes. Paul reminded Timothy of what he suffered during his missionary journeys. God rescued Paul over and over. Eventually, Paul was martyred. Even though persecution will come, God is faithful.

I may not have suffered persecution like Paul yet, but I shouldn't be surprised if it happens. I live in the Kingdom.

Moderation

Aristotle[2] is famous for advocating the "Golden Mean" in philosophy, namely, the middle between two extremes is the desirable way to live.

Ecclesiastes 7:15–20 (CSB)

---

15 In my futile life I have seen everything: someone righteous perishes in spite of his righteousness, and someone wicked lives long in spite of his evil. 16 Don't be excessively righteous, and don't be overly wise. Why should you destroy yourself? 17 Don't be excessively wicked, and don't be foolish. Why should you die before your time? 18 It is good that you grasp the one and do not let the other slip from your hand. For the one who fears God will end up with both of them.

19 Wisdom makes the wise person stronger
than ten rulers of a city.
20 There is certainly no one righteous on the earth
who does good and never sins.

This passage begins with the personal action, "I have seen everything." The prose ends recommending the fear of God followed by a couple of proverbs.

Under the sun. I have seen scoundrels seem to prosper in life. I have seen perfectionists twist life into pretzels. I have seen academics burn out trying to be the world's top expert in their field.

An Israelite might have assumed God rewards righteous living with long life and judges wickedness with a short life. However, the Teacher observed that this is not always so. Trying to be perfectly righteous results in legalism. Trying to be exceedingly wise is exhausting.[3] A wicked lifestyle is foolish and subject to God's judgment. Fearing God is the foundation to understanding

---

[2] Aristotle (384–322 BC) was a pagan Greek philosopher who was very influential on Western Civilization.
[3] Many commentators have difficulty with 7:16–17, because these verses seem to undercut righteous living. Shaw, pp. 102–103.

both wisdom and wickedness. A wise life of moderation is certainly recommended, even though there is no one under the sun who never sins.

I could be a perfectionist. I could be so driven that I burn out. But to fear God and to live moderately sounds much better than extremes. I live under the sun.

In the Kingdom. When I realized that I was a sinner and trying to be a good boy would not get me into heaven, I believed the gospel and was forgiven.

> The righteousness of God is through faith in Jesus Christ to all who believe, since there is no distinction. For all have sinned and fall short of the glory of God; they are justified freely by his grace through the redemption that is in Christ Jesus.
>
> Romans 3:22–24 (CSB)

The New Testament agrees with the Teacher that there is no one who never sins. However, God graciously offers forgiveness and righteousness through faith in Jesus.

I found out human effort trying to be good is never good enough. But God's grace is enough for anyone. I live in the Kingdom.

Ignoring what people say

People give me many opportunities to criticize. Someone may sin. Someone may do something foolish. Someone may make a mistake. Someone may criticize me.

Ecclesiastes 7:21–22 (CSB)

---

21 Don't pay attention to everything people say, or you may hear your servant cursing you, 22 for in your heart you know that many times you yourself have cursed others.

This brief passage gives wise advice.

Under the sun. College students get to rate their teachers at the end of the semester. As a teacher, I didn't like it when an anonymous evaluation gave me a bad grade.

It is best to ignore what people say about you. Someone may curse you. You can't be judgmental of those who criticize you when you have criticized others yourself. The Teacher's advice is hard to put into practice.

Ignoring criticism seems impossible. My natural reaction is to defend myself. When someone does something foolish that inconveniences me, my natural reaction is to criticize. I live under the sun.

In the Kingdom. When I am criticized, I examine myself to see whether I should repent and apologize. Frequently, criticism is baseless, so I just go on with life.

> Conduct yourselves honorably among the [pagans], so that when they slander you as evildoers, they will observe your good works and will glorify God on the day he visits.
>
> 1 Peter 2:12 (CSB)

Believers expect to be cursed and slandered by the world because of the gospel message. For example, the Romans denigrated Christians as "atheists," because they would not participate in civic festivals to worship their pantheon of gods. Peter advised believers to behave righteously, so the pagans will honor them when Jesus returns.

It is still good advice to ignore what people say. Instead of worrying about criticism, I should seek opportunities to do good to others, even to those who criticize me. I live in the Kingdom.

Reaching for wisdom

The guy on TV was supposed to be an expert on politics. If his predictions last election were wrong, why should I believe him this time?

Ecclesiastes 7:23–24 (CSB)

---

23 I have tested all this by wisdom. I resolved, "I will be wise," but it was beyond me. 24 What exists is beyond reach and very deep. Who can discover it?

The beginning of this passage is marked by the personal action, "I have tested all this by wisdom." The last sentence refers to the wisdom one sees in God's creation.

Under the sun. I tried to become an academic expert. I studied in school. I read what experts had to say. I published research in academic journals, but every research paper had a paragraph at the end listing questions that no one knew the answers to.

The Teacher decided that becoming wise was good to do, but he discovered complete wisdom was unobtainable.

In academia, I gained in-depth knowledge of a few things. It is taking a lifetime of experience to gain some common sense. I live under the sun.

In the Kingdom. When I was debugging a software program, I grew frustrated. I couldn't find the bug. Then I remembered James' advice and prayed for insight. What should I do next? God answered my prayer and the solution became evident in a few minutes.

> Now if any of you lacks wisdom, he should ask God—who gives to all generously and ungrudgingly—and it will be given to him.
>
> James 1:5 (CSB)

The Teacher reached for wisdom. God gave him some, but he found complete understanding is beyond human ability. God offers wisdom to any believer who asks. He will supply whatever is needed for the situation. He is generous to all.

God has supplied me with creative ideas to cope with various situations. "Thinking outside the box" is the Creator's specialty. I live in the Kingdom.

Avoiding schemes

Anybody with some common sense knows sin has bad consequences and pranks will backfire. If a friend concocts some foolish scheme, I know to get away as fast as I can.

Ecclesiastes 7:25–29 (CSB)

---

25 I turned my thoughts to know, explore, and examine wisdom and an explanation for things, and to know that wickedness is stupidity and folly is madness. 26 And I find more bitter than death the woman who is a trap: her heart a net and her hands chains. The one who pleases God will escape her, but the sinner will be captured by her. 27 "Look," says the Teacher, "I have discovered this by adding one thing to another to find out the explanation, 28 which my soul continually searches for but does not find: I found one person in a thousand, but none of those was a woman.

29 "Only see this: I have discovered that God made people upright, but they pursued many schemes."

The beginning of this passage is marked by personal action, "I turned my thoughts." The end is marked by God's actions in contrast to those of people.

Under the sun. Some of my friends thought getting drunk or high was fun, but addiction resulted in broken family relationships, expulsion from college, and loss of employment.

This passage argues that it is stupid to pursue sin and folly. Some commentators consider the woman in this passage to be a metaphor for folly,[4] similar

---

[4] *UBS Old Testament Handbook, s.v.* 7:26.

to the advice in Proverbs 5:1–14 to avoid a seductive adulteress. Intimacy with her is a trap for sinners. Understanding this was difficult for the Teacher. Even though God made Adam perfect in the Garden of Eden, people today seek wicked schemes.

Sin and foolishness may seem like fun at the time, but the consequences can ruin life and even lead to premature death. I live under the sun.

In the Kingdom. I carefully explained the gospel to the guy down the hall in the college dorm. He rejected it. I suppose he did not want to change the trajectory of his life.

> This is the judgment: The light has come into the world, and people loved darkness rather than the light because their deeds were evil. For everyone who does evil hates the light and avoids it, so that his deeds may not be exposed.
>
> John 3:19–20 (CSB)

When Jesus came into the world, his ministry exposed evil schemes. He was rejected then and is rejected today because people love evil and do not want to be exposed. The gospel message offers forgiveness and a life in the light. I live in the Kingdom.

A bright face

The cosmetics industry has a thousand and one products to counteract the effects of worry. Understanding puts a smile and a relaxed look on a face.

Ecclesiastes 8:1 (CSB)

---

1 Who is like the wise person, and who knows the interpretation of a matter? A person's wisdom brightens his face, and the sternness of his face is changed.

This brief passage concludes this major section.

Under the sun. While I was teaching a class, I asked everyone a question. There were puzzled looks. Some students stared at the slide on the screen. Some stared at their notes. Then one student smiled and raised a hand.

Wisdom has a positive effect on a person's countenance.

When I was in high school, I didn't need to raise my hand when I knew the answer to the teacher's question. She could see it on my face. I live under the sun.

In the Kingdom. Faye seemed to smile all the time. Even near the end of her life when the pain of cancer wracked her body, visitors said they felt cheered by her smile. She had the hope, joy, and peace God provides.

> Now may the God of hope fill you with all joy and peace as you believe so that you may overflow with hope by the power of the Holy Spirit.
>
> Romans 15:13 (CSB)

A believer has hope which spills out of his face with joy and peace. The Holy Spirit energizes, so that hope touches all of life.

As I walked down the sidewalk, I smiled at each person I met and often said, "Good morning!" God's joy was splashing out, and a smile is contagious. I live in the Kingdom.

11

Authority

I am under the authority of government officials, the management at work, the leaders at church, and in community organizations. I have to remind myself that those in authority over me are human. Sometimes they make mistakes and sometimes they sin.

Obeying the king

In ancient times, the authority of a king was absolute, and the word of a king was law. Because we don't have such kings today, the Teacher's advice seems remote.

Ecclesiastes 8:2–8 (CSB)

---

2 Keep the king's command because of your oath made before God. 3 Do not be in a hurry; leave his presence, and don't persist in a bad cause, since he will do whatever he wants. 4 For the king's word is authoritative, and who can say to him, "What are you doing?" 5 The one who keeps a command will not experience anything harmful, and a wise heart knows the right time and procedure.

6 For every activity there is a right time and procedure, even though a person's troubles are heavy on him. 7 Yet no one knows what will happen because who can tell him what will happen? 8 No one has authority over the wind to restrain it, and there is no authority over the day of death; no one is discharged during battle, and wickedness will not allow those who practice it to escape.

This passage gives advice to officials who work for the king.

Under the sun. When my boss told me to falsify my timecard with the wrong account number, which is illegal, I had to follow proper protocol. With his approval, I informed him of all the true timecard information without actually filling it out or signing it. I assume he falsified my timecard and signed it himself.

The Teacher recommended doing whatever the king commands, because the official had sworn an oath before God to be loyal to the king. The Teacher counseled one to be wise when dealing with the king. For example, do not react hastily to the king's commands, and do not persist in a matter the king opposes. The wise official will follow correct law, protocol, and timing when advising the king.

The second paragraph applies to an official, but also applies to anyone. Godly principles and wise timing will sustain one in troubled seasons of life. The wise person acknowledges he doesn't know the future. For example, no one controls the wind,[1] nor controls when he will die. Moreover, the wise recognizes that sin does not provide an escape from this uncertainty and one's personal responsibilities.

Most nations today do not have leaders who are absolute rulers. However, every boss has some authority over those working for him. The Teacher's advice for an official applies to my employee situations. I live under the sun.

In the Kingdom. Persecution of Christians in China varies from place to place and time to time. National officials oppose Christianity, but sometimes local officials see the good things Christians do for the community, so they don't bother them.

> Submit to every human authority because of the Lord, whether to the emperor as the supreme authority or to governors as those sent out by him to punish those who do what is evil and to praise those who do what is good. For it is God's will that you silence the ignorance of foolish people by doing good.
>
> 1 Peter 2:13–15 (CSB)

The New Testament teaches believers to submit to secular governing authority. The pagans criticized the Christians, but their good works in the community were their answer.

> Come now, you who say, "Today or tomorrow we will travel to such and such a city and spend a year there and do business and make a profit." Yet you do not know what tomorrow will bring—what your life will be! For you are like vapor that appears for a little while, then vanishes.
>
> Instead, you should say, "If the Lord wills, we will live and do this or that."
>
> James 4:13–15 (CSB)

---

[1] The Hebrew word *ruach* (*Strong's* No. 7307) translated *wind* also means *life-breath* or *spirit*.

The Teacher acknowledged the uncertainty of life. Similarly, James taught believers to submit their plans to the will of God, and not to arrogantly assume they are in control of the future.

As a young professional, I went to a seminar that recommended setting goals for my life. "What do you want to be doing in five years?" I knew that God guides my career, so I didn't try to set such goals. When I felt God wanted me to teach at a college, I knew I needed an advanced degree to qualify. So I applied to graduate school. God led me step by step through my career change. I live in the Kingdom.

Wicked authority

Angie had a boss who always seemed to rant about everything. What happens when someone in authority abuses those under him?

Ecclesiastes 8:9–10 (CSB)

---

9 All this I have seen, applying my mind to all the work that is done under the sun, at a time when one person has authority over another to his harm.

10 In such circumstances, I saw the wicked buried. They came and went from the holy place, and they were praised in the city where they did those things. This too is futile.

The beginning of this passage is marked by the personal action, "All this I have seen." The end is marked by declaring this too is vanity. The Hebrew text of verse 10 is uncertain.[2]

Under the sun. My university had a president who did not embrace the culture of the institution. For example, he ordered pulling up flowers that were loved by everyone. After a short tenure, he left for a job in politics.

In this passage, the Teacher focused on when a person in authority oppressed those under him. When he died and was buried, people forgot his wickedness and praised him. The Teacher concluded this is vanity.

Sometimes a boss mistreats his employees. After he is gone, his memory is vanity. I live under the sun.

In the Kingdom. I visited a large church which had a well known guest speaker that Sunday. He refused a customary honorarium. He said his home church paid him well enough and they encouraged him to speak other places.

---

[2]The spelling of the Hebrew word translated *praised* is uncertain. It could mean *forgotten*. Shaw, pp. 116–117. Wright, p. 1179.

I exhort the elders among you as a fellow elder and witness to the
sufferings of Christ, as well as one who shares in the glory about
to be revealed: Shepherd God's flock among you, not overseeing
out of compulsion but willingly, as God would have you; not out of
greed for money but eagerly; not lording it over those entrusted to
you, but being examples to the flock. And when the chief Shepherd
appears, you will receive the unfading crown of glory.

1 Peter 5:1–4 (CSB)

In the world, those in authority often oppress those under them. Those in
authority among Christians (for example, bishops, priests, pastors, and elders)
are not to rule like the world does, but are to be examples to the flock. They are
to serve willingly, eagerly, and without lording over others.

My employer sponsored leadership seminars which were conducted by experts. I found the world's leadership style is different from leading by example. The world operates through greed and control of others. Whenever I'm
pressed into a leadership role, I must have pure motives, because I live in the
Kingdom.

Inevitable justice

"Justice delayed is justice denied," is a maxim attributed to William Gladstone
(1809–1898), a British statesman.[3]

Ecclesiastes 8:11–13 (CSB)

---

11 Because the sentence against an evil act is not carried out quickly,
the heart of people is filled with the desire to commit evil. 12 Although a sinner does evil a hundred times and prolongs his life,
I also know that it will go well with God-fearing people, for they
are reverent before him. 13 However, it will not go well with the
wicked, and they will not lengthen their days like a shadow, for
they are not reverent before God.

This passage explains that God's justice is inevitable even though evil people seems to escape at first.

Under the sun. Many cold criminal cases are being solved years later using
modern DNA technology.[4] Old DNA from the crime scene can be matched to
a genealogy database, leading to the culprit.

---

[3]Martin Luther King, Jr. (1929–1968), an American civil rights leader, paraphrased the quote in
his "Letter from Birmingham Jail" (1963).

[4]Robert Gearty, "DNA, genetic genealogy helping to solve the coldest of cold cases," *Fox News*,
February 5, 2020. Available at https://www.foxnews.com/us/dna-genetic-genealogy-helping-to-
solve-the-coldest-of-cold-cases (Current November 1, 2020).

One is disappointed when the legal sentence against a crime is delayed. The Teacher recognized other criminals may think they can get away with their crimes. What does God think about sin? Even if sin is a lifelong pattern, a long life is not a sign of divine approval. It will not go well for the sinner in the end. In contrast, God blesses those who fear him.

Human justice may be delayed because of legal maneuvers or because the investigation goes cold without finding the perpetrator. But God's justice will always prevail in the end. I live under the sun.

In the Kingdom. When I do something wrong, I don't always recognize it as sin for a while, especially if it is my established behavior pattern. I am thankful God gives me time to see my actions the way he sees them, so I can repent. Then the Holy Spirit helps me change my patterns.

> The Lord does not delay his promise, as some understand delay, but is patient with you, not wanting any to perish but all to come to repentance.
>
> 2 Peter 3:9 (CSB)

Sometimes we wonder why God is letting the evil in this world get worse and worse. Why doesn't Jesus just come back today to establish righteousness? The answer is God is giving people time to repent.

> [The pagans] will give an account to the one who stands ready to judge the living and the dead.
>
> 1 Peter 4:5 (CSB)

God promises that his justice is inevitable. Everyone is accountable for what he has done, standing before King Jesus. I am always aware of God's justice and his mercy. I live in the Kingdom.

Injustice

In America, a District Attorney at the local level is often elected. This office is the main prosecutor for state-level crimes. Justice is corrupted when the person in this office prosecutes an innocent person because it will help him get reelected.

Ecclesiastes 8:14 (CSB)

---

14 There is a futility that is done on the earth: there are righteous people who get what the actions of the wicked deserve, and there are wicked people who get what the actions of the righteous deserve. I say that this too is futile.

This passage is bracketed by the word *futility* (CSB), namely, vanity.

Under the sun. Some people have "kick-the-dog syndrome" when they are angry and frustrated. The master comes home fuming about what just happened and kicks the loving family dog in anger. Sadly, sometimes the victim is a child.

The Teacher admitted that injustice happens in human affairs. Sometimes the government's justice system convicts an innocent person instead of the true perpetrator of a crime. Sometimes the media commend the criminal instead of the innocent person.

It often takes a lifetime to learn to control anger and properly channel frustrations. I live under the sun.

In the Kingdom. Christians are falsely accused and prosecuted in many parts of the world. Anyone may suffer routine injustice, just because people in authority sin. A Christian may suffer injustice specifically because of loyalty to Jesus.

> But if anyone suffers as a Christian, let him not be ashamed but let him glorify God in having that name.
>
> 1 Peter 4:16 (CSB)

Peter warned believers to expect to suffer injustice for being Christians. Instead of being discouraged, one should praise God for the privilege of representing Christ who also suffered injustice.

Some of my atheist friends have strong opinions. I try to avoid arguments on social media, but when conflict happens, I must respond in a godly way. I live in the Kingdom.

Enjoying life

Even though a boss may make bad decisions or oppress the employees and even though there may be no avenue for redress, one can still find enjoyable things in life.

Ecclesiastes 8:15 (CSB)

---

15 So I commended enjoyment because there is nothing better for a person under the sun than to eat, drink, and enjoy himself, for this will accompany him in his labor during the days of his life that God gives him under the sun.

This passage marks the end of the major section on authority by recommending enjoyment of life. The beginning of the passage is marked by the personal action, "So I commended." The end is marked by God's action.

Under the sun. I usually left the office to have lunch. If the office was close to home, I would have lunch there. If not close, I would often find a quiet place alone.

Even though there are wicked oppressive authorities and even though there are injustices, the Teacher recommended enjoying life as one works. He acknowledged that however long one lives, it is the gift of God.

An oppressive boss or injustice at the office does not have to intrude on enjoying my lunch. I live under the sun.

In the Kingdom. One way I maintain a quiet life is to limit my activity on social media. My occasional posts are not controversial and my privacy settings are strict.

> Seek to lead a quiet life, to mind your own business, and to work with your own hands, as we commanded you, so that you may behave properly in the presence of outsiders and not be dependent on anyone.
>
> 1 Thessalonians 4:11–12 (CSB)

Paul recommended that believers lead a quiet life insofar as it depends on them. Daily life consists of honest work and behavior, without depending on those outside the faith.

My faith is obvious but not aggressive. My social media strategy helps me focus on important things in the Kingdom. I live in the Kingdom.

12

Expecting death

Death is part of the natural order. Young adults are famous for acting as if they are immortal. A wise person acknowledges his mortality and lives accordingly.

Observing God's works

The Merritt Island National Wildlife Refuge is famous among bird watchers. It is a wetland that attracts a huge variety of exotic birds—and alligators! Observing God's works is why I visit.

Ecclesiastes 8:16–17 (CSB)

16 When I applied my mind to know wisdom and to observe the activity that is done on the earth (even though one's eyes do not close in sleep day or night), 17 I observed all the work of God and concluded that a person is unable to discover the work that is done under the sun. Even though a person labors hard to explore it, he cannot find it; even if a wise person claims to know it, he is unable to discover it.

The previous passage recommended enjoying life. That made it the end of a section, so this passage is the beginning of a new section. The beginning of this passage is marked by the personal action, "I applied my mind."

Under the sun. Astronomy photos from the Hubble telescope are beautiful; then you find out how big and how far away those clouds of stars are—amazing. I was shocked the first time I looked in a microscope and saw tiny creatures God made. The variety of God's creation is mind-boggling.

The Teacher carefully observed creation and everything else God does under the sun. Only a fraction can be comprehended, no matter how diligent one is to discover everything.

The regular visitors to my backyard are amazing: butterflies, birds, lizards, squirrels, and raccoons. Understanding everything is certainly impossible. I live under the sun.

In the Kingdom. In high school, I had to evaluate what I was reading against the Bible's teaching. History class assumed people are basically good, but the Bible tells me people are sinners. Novels in English class presented sexual immorality as acceptable, but the Bible tells me it is sin.

> Do not be conformed to this age, but be transformed by the renewing of your mind, so that you may discern what is the good, pleasing, and perfect will of God.
>
> Romans 12:2 (CSB)

It is not necessary to understand all that God does. It is only necessary to understand God's will for today. This happens when one's mind is transformed from the world's way of thinking to God's way. Then one can discern God's will and what pleases him.

As I have grown spiritually, my mind has been renewed. Thought patterns were reinforced as I studied the Bible and critically evaluated what worldly voices said. More and more, I've been able to recognize truth, justice, and righteousness. I live from day to day in the Kingdom.

Everyone's fate

Thousands may mourn the death of a famous person. The funeral may be on TV. A small graveside service may be the memorial for a poor veteran with no family. The celebrations may be different, but both have the same fate.

Ecclesiastes 9:1–3 (CSB)

---

1 Indeed, I took all this to heart and explained it all: The righteous, the wise, and their works are in God's hands. People don't know whether to expect love or hate. Everything lies ahead of them. 2 Everything is the same for everyone: There is one fate for the righteous and the wicked, for the good and the bad, for the clean and the unclean, for the one who sacrifices and the one who does not sacrifice. As it is for the good, so also it is for the sinner; as it is for the one who takes an oath, so also for the one who fears an oath. 3 This is an evil in all that is done under the sun: there is one fate for everyone.

The beginning of this passage, is marked by the personal action, "Indeed, I took all this to heart and explained it all." The end is marked by the declaration, "This is an evil," in other words, vanity.

Under the sun. Attending funerals is a part of my life. Each one celebrates the life of the deceased in a special way. There is grieving and there is comfort for the living. Precious memories are shared. The deceased may have had a long life, or life may have been cut short by tragedy. Whatever the circumstances, everyone dies.

The lives of wise righteous people are in God's control, not their own control. No one knows the future in life, but one thing is certain: everyone dies. This truth is illustrated by a list of contrasting pairs of people. The destiny of death is not affected by the life one lives. The Teacher concluded this is vanity.

Most of us don't meditate on death the way the Teacher did. When I paused to think about it, the reality of my future death slapped me. I tried to imagine what will happen when I die. I realized my family would have a mess on their hands. So I am simplifying my stuff so they won't have to untangle such a mess. I live under the sun.

In the Kingdom. Faye had terminal cancer. The doctors were sure it would take her life. Because she was a believer, she was not afraid of death. Her Christian friends had a hard time accepting the medical facts, but she kept explaining her unshakable hope for eternal life.

It is appointed for people to die once—and after this, judgment.
Hebrews 9:27 (CSB)

Like the Teacher, the New Testament acknowledges everyone's life ends in death. Moreover, after death, at the end of the age, all will face judgment for what they have done.

God guarantees death and judgment are coming, but as a citizen of the Kingdom, I do not need to fear death. My sins are forgiven. I live in the Kingdom.

Knowing I will die

Ancient cultures put clothes, tools, riches, and food in the grave with a deceased person thinking they would be useful in the afterlife. Grave robbers often got the valuables. Archaeologists found whatever was left thousands of years later. The dead never benefited.

Ecclesiastes 9:3–6 (CSB)

In addition, the hearts of people are full of evil, and madness is in their hearts while they live; after that they go to the dead. 4 But there is hope for whoever is joined with all the living, since a live dog is better than a dead lion. 5 For the living know that they will die, but the dead don't know anything. There is no longer a reward for them because the memory of them is forgotten. 6 Their love, their hate, and their envy have already disappeared, and there is no longer a portion for them in all that is done under the sun.

This passage continues the discussion of death. The end is marked by a reference to "all that is done under the sun."

Under the sun. A bumper sticker says, "He who dies with the most toys wins." People collect big toys as they get older. My toys and hobbies won't benefit me after I die.

People are sinners and generally foolish. Then they die. The Teacher saw that the dead don't have any benefits under the sun. No one remembers their actions or feelings. At least the living know they will die in the future.

My love, hate, and envy won't matter to anyone after I'm gone. Knowing I will die is a sobering thought. I live under the sun.

In the Kingdom. To mark my spiritual progress, I ask myself some questions. Do my actions produce good spiritual fruit? Do I understand God's ways? Do I handle difficult circumstances in a godly way? Am I thankful?

> [We are asking God] that you may walk worthy of the Lord, fully pleasing to him: bearing fruit in every good work and growing in the knowledge of God, being strengthened with all power, according to his glorious might, so that you may have great endurance and patience, joyfully giving thanks to the Father, who has enabled you to share in the saints' inheritance in the light.
>
> Colossians 1:10–12 (CSB)

Instead of sin and foolishness, believers have a mission in life. Paul prayed for the Colossians that they would live worthy of the Lord, pleasing him. This includes doing good works, knowing God more and more, becoming spiritually strong, having endurance, and giving thanks to God. Instead of only an inheritance under the sun while alive, believers have an eternal inheritance.

My spiritual maturity is measured by the qualities listed in these verses. After this life, I will share in an eternal inheritance. I live in the Kingdom.

Enjoying life

I saw a t-shirt that said, "Life is short. Eat dessert first."[1]

---

[1]There are hundreds of quotes and slogans that begin with "Life is short" or "Life is too short."

Ecclesiastes 9:7–10 (CSB)

---

7 Go, eat your bread with pleasure, and drink your wine with a cheerful heart, for God has already accepted your works. 8 Let your clothes be white all the time, and never let oil be lacking on your head. 9 Enjoy life with the wife you love all the days of your fleeting [futile] life, which has been given to you under the sun, all your fleeting days. For that is your portion in life and in your struggle under the sun. 10 Whatever your hands find to do, do with all your strength, because there is no work, planning, knowledge, or wisdom in Sheol where you are going.

This passage concludes the major section on expecting death by recommending enjoyment of life. In verse 9, the CSB expression *fleeting life* could also be translated *futile life*, namely a life of vanity. *Sheol* is the Hebrew word for the place of the dead, which the CSB does not translate.

Under the sun. Life has its enjoyable moments. I'm not a gourmet, but I enjoy the flavors of every meal. My wife helped me shop for professional attire when I worked for accountants, and I shave every day whether I like it or not. I love my wife. Weeding in the backyard may not be fun, but I like the result.

Even though the wise person knows death is inevitable, the Teacher recommended enjoying life. Enjoy what you eat and drink. Enjoy presentable clothes and being well groomed. Enjoy loving your spouse. Pursue your work diligently. None of these things in life happen after one dies.

Instead of dwelling on my death, I'm enjoying life. I'm following the Teacher's advice. I live under the sun.

In the Kingdom. The New Testament agrees with the Teacher that a healthy marriage is desirable and honored.

> Marriage is to be honored by all and the marriage bed kept undefiled, because God will judge the sexually immoral and adulterers.
> Hebrews 13:4 (CSB)

My marriage to Angie has been a joy these many years. Our love for each other has its foundation on our mutual love for God. Putting Kingdom principles into practice has helped us grow personally and spiritually.

Pulling weeds in the backyard may not seem like a spiritual activity, but it creates a pleasing environment that is a gift to the neighbors, and that means pulling weeds is one way to love my neighbors.

> And whatever you do, in word or in deed, do everything in the name of the Lord Jesus, giving thanks to God the Father through him.
> Colossians 3:17 (CSB)

Rather than working just for self satisfaction under the sun, a believer is diligent to do every activity of life in the name of Jesus. Everything is done with a thankful heart.

Every activity I do under the sun is transformed into the Kingdom when my motive is to give Jesus credit. During every activity under the sun, I will thank God for his grace in every detail of life. I live in the Kingdom.

13

Time and chance

A baseball batter tries to hit a round ball with a round bat. No one can be sure where the ball will go—unless he misses altogether. Many things in life are unpredictable.

Ecclesiastes 9:11–12 (CSB)

---

11 Again I saw under the sun that the race is not to the swift, or the battle to the strong, or bread to the wise, or riches to the discerning, or favor to the skillful; rather, time and chance happen to all of them. 12 For certainly no one knows his time: like fish caught in a cruel net or like birds caught in a trap, so people are trapped in an evil time as it suddenly falls on them.

This passage has a distinct topic compared to the major sections before and after, so it is a brief major section in the outline. The beginning of this passage is marked by the personal action, "Again I saw under the sun."

Under the sun. When I began my career, I had great hopes of helping mankind. After working a short while, I saw limitations on what I could accomplish in a corporate context. I thought about becoming a consultant, but I realized running a business was much more than just consulting.

One would think that those with good personal qualities would always benefit in life. The Teacher listed athletic ability, strength, wisdom, discernment, and skill. However, there are no guarantees in life. Just as a fish gets caught in a net or a bird gets trapped by chance, disaster can fall on anyone. "Time and chance happen to all."

There are unknowable unknowns in any career. Sometimes disaster falls. Some projects I worked on turned out to be failures. I live under the sun.

In the Kingdom. When you read the news, there is plenty to worry about. In 2020, the news media said the stores were out of toilet paper! Jesus said, "Don't worry!" so I focused on the Kingdom and I had enough toilet paper.

> [Jesus said:] Therefore I tell you: Don't worry about your life, what you will eat or what you will drink; or about your body, what you will wear. Isn't life more than food and the body more than clothing? ... For the Gentiles eagerly seek all these things, and your heavenly Father knows that you need them. But seek first the kingdom of God and his righteousness, and all these things will be provided for you. Therefore don't worry about tomorrow, because tomorrow will worry about itself. Each day has enough trouble of its own.
>
> Matthew 6:25–34 (CSB)

When disaster strikes, it is easy to be discouraged. Jesus said, "Don't worry!" In this passage, Jesus illustrated his point. God feeds the birds and he clothes the wild flowers. The pagans look for safety, but believers know God cares about them. So, a believer's priority is to live in the Kingdom.

14

Characteristics of fools

If I don't want to be a fool, I should find out what to avoid. This section is largely proverbs on characteristics of fools compared to characteristics of the wise.

> But know this: Hard times will come in the last days. For people will be lovers of self, lovers of money, boastful, proud, demeaning, disobedient to parents, ungrateful, unholy, unloving, irreconcilable, slanderers, without self-control, brutal, without love for what is good, traitors, reckless, conceited, lovers of pleasure rather than lovers of God, holding to the form of godliness but denying its power. Avoid these people.
>
> 2 Timothy 3:1–5 (CSB)

Paul warned Timothy that people's morals were going to get worse and worse, especially just before Jesus returns. The list of sinful attitudes goes on and on. Some will be religious, professing to be Christians, but denying God's power in daily life. Paul's list seems to describe modern life under the sun precisely.

Wisdom despised

Many people cling to their opinions even when refuted by logic and facts. In order to continue advancing their illogical arguments modern fools have to pretend not to know things.[1]

Ecclesiastes 9:13–10:1 (CSB)

---

13 I have observed that this also is wisdom under the sun, and it is significant to me: 14 There was a small city with few men in it.

---

[1] Paraphrase of a quote attributed to American playwright David Mamet.

A great king came against it, surrounded it, and built large siege works against it. 15 Now a poor wise man was found in the city, and he delivered the city by his wisdom. Yet no one remembered that poor man. 16 And I said, "Wisdom is better than strength, but the wisdom of the poor man is despised, and his words are not heeded."

> 17 The calm words of the wise are heeded
> more than the shouts of a ruler over fools.
> 18 Wisdom is better than weapons of war,
> but one sinner can destroy much good.
> 1 Dead flies make a perfumer's oil ferment and stink;
> so a little folly outweighs wisdom and honor.

The beginning of this passage is marked by the personal action, " I have observed." The prose parable is followed by three proverbs.

Under the sun. I met a war protester as I was walking across my college campus. I tried to engage him in a conversation, but he just kept saying slogans.

The Teacher told a parable to illustrate how wisdom is often despised by the public. A city was attacked and surrounded. Hope was lost. But the wisdom of a poor man saved the city. Afterward, the people forgot about the poor man and ignored his wisdom because he was poor.

The first proverb points out that fools shout, trying to win an argument, but the calm words of the wise are more effective.

The second proverb reminds one of how the wise poor man saved the city, but just one sinner can wreck good plans.

The third proverb gives an analogy. Dead flies in ointment are like the wreckage caused by the one sinner in the previous proverb. The public thinks his foolishness is better than wisdom.

A modern executive's selfish ambitions resulted in poor business decisions. The Wall Street pundits praised him for his "bold vision," but later everyone saw the disastrous consequences. Fools despise wisdom. I live under the sun.

In the Kingdom. At a typical elite university, only a tiny minority of faculty are believers, if any. You are more likely to find believers among the janitors and food service workers. At my university, when a small group of students wanted to pray, the food service department let them use a storage room. Other places were not available.

> Brothers and sisters, consider your calling: Not many were wise from a human perspective, not many powerful, not many of noble birth. Instead, God has chosen what is foolish in the world to shame the wise, and God has chosen what is weak in the world to shame the strong. God has chosen what is insignificant and despised in

the world—what is viewed as nothing—to bring to nothing what is viewed as something, so that no one may boast in his presence.

1 Corinthians 1:26–29 (CSB)

The Christians in Corinth mostly came from the lower classes. There were few philosophers, scholars, military leaders, politicians, or nobility. God's grace was received by the poor and uneducated. They received God's wisdom and understanding of spiritual truths.

God's wisdom is often despised by those living only under the sun. The rich and famous may despise Christians, but those in a little country church have God-given common sense and spiritual insight. I live in the Kingdom.

Footsteps of fools

In America, we drive on the right side of the road. If I stay to the right, I will be safe. If I stray to the left, I may meet oncoming traffic head-on.

Ecclesiastes 10:2–4 (CSB)

---

2 A wise person's heart goes to the right,
but a fool's heart to the left.
3 Even when the fool walks along the road, his heart lacks sense,
and he shows everyone he is a fool.
4 If the ruler's anger rises against you, don't leave your post,
for calmness puts great offenses to rest.

This passage consists of a series of three proverbs.

Under the sun. Driving in traffic seems to bring out foolishness in people. The guy behind me was impatient going the speed limit, so he zoomed around me, sped ahead to wait at the red light, while I came up behind him. His reckless maneuver gained him one car length.

The Teacher's first proverb compares the heart tendencies of a wise person and a fool. The fool turns toward trouble, represented by the left side of a path.

The second proverb says even if a fool is walking correctly down a path, he still acts foolishly. Everyone can see it.

In the third proverb, a fool will run away when the ruler is angry, but a wise person will stay at his post and react with a calm demeanor.

I try to recognize when someone around me is acting foolishly. I'll give such a person plenty of room, so I don't get involved in his schemes. I live under the sun.

In the Kingdom. When I recognize sinful actions and attitudes, I know deadly consequences are ahead.

> If we walk in the light as [God] himself is in the light, we have fellowship with one another, and the blood of Jesus his Son cleanses us from all sin.
>
> 1 John 1:7 (CSB)

When believers live according to Kingdom principles and in fellowship with God and other Christians, they remain cleansed from sin.

Living in the Kingdom is like walking in light. Biblical principles give me insight into people and situations. Spending time with other believers helps me stay balanced and encouraged. I live in the Kingdom.

Foolish officials

Sometimes the boss appoints an unqualified person to a responsible position. After a short while, his incompetence becomes obvious to all the workers.

Ecclesiastes 10:5–7 (CSB)

---

5 There is an evil I have seen under the sun, an error proceeding from the presence of the ruler:

> 6 The fool is appointed to great heights,
> but the rich remain in lowly positions.
> 7 I have seen slaves on horses,
> but princes walking on the ground like slaves.

The beginning of this passage is marked by the personal action, "There is an evil I have seen under the sun." The introductory sentence sets the scene, and is followed by two proverbs about officials.

Under the sun. The Peter Principle asserts people in a hierarchy tend to be promoted to their level of incompetence.[2] I've often wondered how a poor manager was ever promoted that high.

The first proverb complains that a fool was appointed to high office, but a rich man was not. One assumes the rich man was more competent.

The second proverb contrasts slaves and princes. Riding a horse is more honored than walking. One assumes a slave does not deserve royal honors, but a prince is trained for royalty from childhood.

The Teacher saw the Peter Principle among government officials in his day. I have seen it among modern officials, too. I live under the sun.

---

[2]Lawrence J. Peter and Raymond Hull, *The Peter Principle* (New York: William Morrow, 1969).

In the Kingdom. A homeless man camped in the woods next to the church for many years. Occasionally, he joined the men for a Saturday breakfast and Bible study. The church people greeted him whenever they saw him on the church property, and welcomed him at services. They didn't expect him to wear Sunday-best clothes.

> My brothers and sisters, do not show favoritism as you hold on to
> the faith in our glorious Lord Jesus Christ.
>
> James 2:1 (CSB)

James carefully explained in this and following verses that believers must not show favoritism. Especially, one should not honor the rich and despise the poor just because of their social class.

Church leadership should be especially careful when appointing leaders within the church. The world looks at external factors like personality, financial contributions, social class, and community connections. Humble godly believers who will be examples to the flock are the leaders Jesus wants. I live in the Kingdom.

Foolish risks

Down the street, the city is putting in a new storm sewer and curbs with drains. They have to dig a deep pit to position the concrete storm sewer pipe. However, the Florida sand keeps sliding into the hole.

Ecclesiastes 10:8–11 (CSB)

---

8 The one who digs a pit may fall into it,
and the one who breaks through a wall may be bitten by a snake.
9 The one who quarries stones may be hurt by them;
the one who splits logs may be endangered by them.
10 If the ax is dull, and one does not sharpen its edge,
then one must exert more strength;
however, the advantage of wisdom is that it brings success.
11 If the snake bites before it is charmed,
then there is no advantage for the charmer.

This passage consists of a series of proverbs about risks in daily life.

Under the sun. When I was a boy, we played in the woods across the street. As I casually walked along a trail, I heard a buzzing sound. A rattlesnake was telling me to go away. So I did.

Sometimes the walls of a pit collapse while one is digging. Sometimes one falls into the pit. Sometimes a snake is hiding at a construction site. Sometimes rocks fall while one works at a quarry. Sometimes pieces of wood fly about when splitting logs. When chopping wood, it is wise to sharpen the ax first. A snake charmer won't be successful if the snake bites him first. The Teacher's implication in all of these is an impetuous fool will suffer, but practical wisdom brings success.

I've been victim of my own foolishness at times. I would never make a good snake charmer. A wise person stays away from snakes. I live under the sun.

In the Kingdom. When I was a teenager, Sunday School class taught me how to interpret the Bible for myself. This has helped me ever since to grow gradually in spiritual maturity.

> We proclaim [Christ], warning and teaching everyone with all wisdom, so that we may present everyone mature in Christ.
>
> Colossians 1:28 (CSB)

Like the Teacher, the New Testament values wisdom, especially godly wisdom, because believers become mature in Christ as they learn about life in the Kingdom.

I'm thankful for the godly men who were my teachers in those formative years. I live in the Kingdom.

Words of a fool

A wise person once said, "Better to remain silent and be thought a fool than to speak and remove all doubt."[3]

Ecclesiastes 10:12–15 (CSB)

---

12 The words from the mouth of a wise person are gracious,
but the lips of a fool consume him.
13 The beginning of the words from his mouth is folly,
but the end of his speaking is evil madness;
14 yet the fool multiplies words.
No one knows what will happen,
and who can tell anyone what will happen after him?
15 The struggles of fools weary them,
for they don't know how to go to the city.

This passage consists of a series of proverbs about things fools say.

[3]This quote is often attributed to Abraham Lincoln, but this is doubtful. Its author is uncertain. https://quoteinvestigator.com/2010/05/17/remain-silent (Current November 1, 2020).

Under the sun. When someone rants about politics, one opinion after another is foisted on those nearby. No one knows who will win the next election. The conversation quickly deteriorates into hatred and foolishness. That's when I quit listening and look for a way out.

A wise person's speech has grace for others, but a fool is destroyed by what he says. A fool's speech is about folly, evil, and foolishness, over and over. The wise person admits no one knows the future, but fools struggle to find their way.

I don't have to listen to foolish ranting either in person or on social media. It never makes sense anyway. I will guard my mind. I live under the sun.

In the Kingdom. Angie taught conversational English to spouses of international students. She had to choose her words carefully, to speak slowly, and to pronounce words clearly. She adjusted how she spoke to the skill level of each person. That was how she demonstrated God's love for them.

> Act wisely toward outsiders, making the most of the time. Let your speech always be gracious, seasoned with salt, so that you may know how you should answer each person.
>
> Colossians 4:5–6 (CSB)

Like the Teacher, Paul recommended gracious speech to the Colossian believers. A wise believer will find the best way to communicate with each person, especially worldly people.

I'm learning to follow Angie's example when I talk with internationals. English is usually their second language. Gracious speech shows God's love to the listener. I live in the Kingdom.

Foolishness of a young king

When electing leaders, each voter must decide: do I want those seeking status and fame, or do I want servants of the public?

Ecclesiastes 10:16–17 (CSB)

---

16 Woe to you, land, when your king is a youth
and your princes feast in the morning.
17 Blessed are you, land, when your king is a son of nobles
and your princes feast at the proper time—
for strength and not for drunkenness.

This passage consists of a pair of proverbs comparing a foolish youthful king with a wise one.

Under the sun. Sometimes the child of a business owner becomes the boss. The new boss may exploit the business for personal status symbols and perquisites. However, I've also seen businesses where the father trained the child, so the child was ready to run the business responsibly.

The Teacher described a young king who partied with his friends, even in the morning, instead of ruling wisely. The young king who had good training celebrated at appropriate times and for good reasons.

I worked in an office with several adult children of the boss. I could see the boss had taken into account the temperament, skills, and education of each one, so they could each be successful in their own way. I live under the sun.

In the Kingdom. I've noticed some folks show up for every church dinner, but rarely come to worship services or Bible studies. I wonder if their commitment to God is as strong as it is to church dinners.

> [False teachers] will be paid back with harm for the harm they have done. They consider it a pleasure to carouse in broad daylight. They are spots and blemishes, delighting in their deceptions while they feast with you.
>
> 2 Peter 2:13 (CSB)

Peter warned about false teachers at length. Like the foolish young king and his friends, the false teachers partied in the daytime. The false teachers also joined Christians at their regular dinners.

Those who only show up for dinner are teaching by their example, but at least they are not responsible for teaching a class. I live in the Kingdom.

Laziness

I used to say, "I'll do such-and-such when I get around to it." Then I was given a round potholder with *TUIT* printed on it. Now I have no excuse; I have a "round TUIT."

Ecclesiastes 10:18–19 (CSB)

---

18 Because of laziness the roof caves in,
and because of negligent hands the house leaks.
19 A feast is prepared for laughter,
and wine makes life happy,
and money is the answer for everything.

This passage consists of a pair of proverbs. The meaning of verse 19 in this context is unclear.[4]

---

[4] *UBS Old Testament Handbook, s.v.* 10:19.

Under the sun. I can be lazy like anyone else. I'm an expert procrastinator. It's easy to put off doing chores or repairs when a fun opportunity arises. When I finally get around to it, the chore is twice as much work.

The first proverb provides an example of the consequences of laziness, "the house leaks." The second proverb, with a touch of irony, indicates what the lazy fool was doing: feasting with laughter, drunkenness, and extravagant living.

It is tempting to go to a party instead of doing home maintenance. I have to remind myself about the consequences of procrastination, so I can keep my priorities straight. I live under the sun.

In the Kingdom. A missionary to the Democratic Republic of the Congo taught at a Bible school in small town. The curriculum emphasized that village pastors should farm like everyone else. This was the opposite of their culture where everyone wanted to be a "big man," supported by the community.

> In fact, when we were with you, this is what we commanded you: "If anyone isn't willing to work, he should not eat."
>
> 2 Thessalonians 3:10 (CSB)

Paul established a practical rule for the Thessalonians. A lazy person was not to be supported by the Christian community.[5]

A worldly person wants to be a "big man," but as a citizen of the Kingdom, I want to be a servant who is willing to work. I live in the Kingdom.

Cursing

A sports announcer didn't know the microphone was on when he made a crude remark which was broadcast across the nation. He was caught by a "hot mike." He had to resign.

Ecclesiastes 10:20 (CSB)

---

20 Do not curse the king even in your thoughts,
and do not curse a rich person even in your bedroom,
for a bird of the sky may carry the message,
and a winged creature may report the matter.

This passage consists of a proverb.

---

[5] Wright, p. 1182.

Under the sun. Whenever I disagreed with something the boss did, it was easy to come up with cynical criticism. I might make up a clever joke.

This proverb advises one not to curse anyone, especially those in authority. A bird reporting secrets is a figurative image.

I quickly learned not to share my cynical thoughts with coworkers. I live under the sun.

In the Kingdom. Angie had prepared a big bowl of spaghetti sauce. When it fell to the floor, every cabinet in the kitchen was splattered with sauce. She exclaimed, "Now, I know I'm saved!" because loud curses didn't come out of her mouth.

> No foul language should come from your mouth, but only what is good for building up someone in need, so that it gives grace to those who hear.
>
> Ephesians 4:29 (CSB)

A believer must be careful about what he says. Cursing and foul language do not help anybody. Godly speech helps the listener.

Being a believer gave Angie a different vocabulary. She lives in the Kingdom.

15

Life under the sun

What is important in life? Having thoroughly investigated the matter, this section summarizes the Teacher's advice to a young person.

Uncertainty

People in Florida must be prepared for hurricanes. During one storm, we lost our electricity. It was not restored until about a week after the storm. We were prepared with a small generator which kept the refrigerator and freezer going, but not the air conditioner. It was like camping in our own house.

Ecclesiastes 11:1–6 (CSB)

1 Send your bread on the surface of the water,
for after many days you may find it.
2 Give a portion to seven or even to eight,
for you don't know what disaster may happen on earth.
3 If the clouds are full, they will pour out rain on the earth;
whether a tree falls to the south or the north,
the place where the tree falls, there it will lie.
4 One who watches the wind will not sow,
and the one who looks at the clouds will not reap.
5 Just as you don't know the path of the wind,
or how bones develop in the womb of a pregnant woman,
so also you don't know the work of God who makes everything.
6 In the morning sow your seed,
and at evening do not let your hand rest,
because you don't know which will succeed,
whether one or the other,
or if both of them will be equally good.

This passage consists of a series of proverbs with advice for coping with uncertainty.

Under the sun. My plans got upset due to sickness. My plan to work by myself became obsolete when I met someone willing to help me. Unknowns in nature interrupted my plans when a hurricane came.

The first two proverbs[1] point out the uncertainty of life. If one prepares, then one is more likely to survive a disaster. In the first proverb, it is unclear what kind of waters the Teacher referred to. Some commentators associate the water with a maritime shipping business.[2] Perhaps "Cast thy bread upon the waters" (KJV) refers to sowing seed on a water-soaked field; ancient Egyptians sowed after a flooded field was drained. The second proverb recommends dividing one's giving among multiple partners to reduce risk.

The next proverbs[3] reflect on unknowns in nature. Will it rain? Which direction will a tree fall in the forest? If someone waits for perfect weather to do his farming, he will never get a crop.[4] What is the path of the wind? How does a baby form in the womb? The conclusion is no one understands all that God does in creation.

In the face of all such uncertainty, the Teacher recommended to keep working,[5] because you don't know which endeavors will succeed and which will fail.

Uncertainty in life is unavoidable. Staying flexible helps me cope with life's surprises. I live under the sun.

In the Kingdom. As Angie got some exercise bicycling through the neighborhood, she stopped to say "Hi!" to a neighbor. Then she found out the neighbor needed encouragement and prayer. God had arranged Angie's appointment.

> For we are his workmanship, created in Christ Jesus for good works, which God prepared ahead of time for us to do.
>
> Ephesians 2:10 (CSB)

In spite of the uncertainties of life, God prepares situations ahead of time, so that believers can do good works in Jesus' name.

My uncle wrote a book about the basics of the faith. It was translated into Chinese. I bought some to give away. Months later, I gave a copy to the wife of a Chinese student who was ready to learn about Christianity. I live in the Kingdom.

---

[1] 11:1–2.
[2] Shaw, pp. 144–145. Wright, p. 1189.
[3] 11:3–5.
[4] Shaw, p. 145.
[5] 11:6.

Being young

When I finished Army Basic Training, I was the most physically fit I have ever been. I was glad the training was over, and I was glad I was healthy and strong.

Ecclesiastes 11:7–10 (CSB)

---

7 Light is sweet,
and it is pleasing for the eyes to see the sun.
8 Indeed, if someone lives many years,
let him rejoice in them all,
and let him remember the days of darkness, since they will be many.
All that comes is futile.
 9 Rejoice, young person, while you are young,
and let your heart be glad in the days of your youth.
And walk in the ways of your heart
and in the desire of your eyes;
but know that for all of these things God will bring you to judgment.
10 Remove sorrow from your heart,
and put away pain from your flesh,
because youth and the prime of life are fleeting.

This passage consists of poetry, giving advice to a young person. The first two verses end declaring all is vanity. In verse 10, the word translated *fleeting* by the CSB is translated *vanity* by the KJV. Thus, the end of the passage is marked by a declaration of vanity.

Under the sun. While I was single, life was flexible with few responsibilities. I enjoyed many activities with my friends. When I married I gained a faithful companion.

In the first two verses, the Teacher recommended rejoicing that one is alive, that one can see the sun. Even though there may be discouraging years, rejoice in all the years one has. Even so, "All that comes is futile," namely, vanity.

In the latter two verses, the Teacher recommended to a young person to rejoice in all one can do while young, but to remember that God will judge everyone's actions. There is less grieving of the soul and fewer physical aches and pains while young, so enjoy the prime of life.

Now that I'm older, I look back and rejoice in all the years God has given me and my wife. I live under the sun.

In the Kingdom. I had been playing only a few years when my first guitar broke. Before I could buy a replacement, a guy at church gave me a very good guitar. I have been playing Christian songs on it ever since. I have tried to apply the parable of the talents with my guitar.

> For it is just like a man about to go on a journey. He called his own servants and entrusted his possessions to them. To one he gave five talents, to another two talents, and to another one talent, depending on each one's ability. Then he went on a journey. Immediately the man who had received five talents went, put them to work, and earned five more...
>
> Matthew 25:14–30 (CSB)

In ancient times, a talent was a unit of weight. By Roman times one talent of silver was an enormous sum of money, about 6,000 times the wages for a day's work. In this parable, the servants who received five and two talents, put the money to work to earn more. The servant who received one talent hid it, so he would not risk losing it in business. When he returned, the master rewarded the first two servants, but severely punished the one who disobeyed.

Jesus told the parable of the talents to illustrate how Christians, like the servants, are accountable for what God has given them. When Jesus returns, those who have obeyed his directions will be commended and rewarded. Those who have squandered what they have been given will be punished, as their actions deserve.

Jesus has entrusted me with many things. There are physical items, money, natural abilities, and spiritual things. I must use them as a faithful servant. Knowing I'm accountable to use what he gives me makes me sensitive to the leading of the Holy Spirit. God is preparing my circumstances so I can do good works. I don't want to miss any opportunities. I live in the Kingdom.

Growing old

Many people turn away from religion when they are teens or twenty-somethings. They think they can wait until old age to reverence their Creator.

Ecclesiastes 12:1–7 (CSB)

---

1 So remember your Creator in the days of your youth:

Before the days of adversity come,
and the years approach when you will say,
"I have no delight in them";
2 before the sun and the light are darkened,
and the moon and the stars,
and the clouds return after the rain;
3 on the day when the guardians of the house tremble,
and the strong men stoop,
the women who grind grain cease because they are few,

and the ones who watch through the windows see dimly,
4 the doors at the street are shut
while the sound of the mill fades;
when one rises at the sound of a bird,
and all the daughters of song grow faint.
5 Also, they are afraid of heights and dangers on the road;
the almond tree blossoms,
the grasshopper loses its spring,
and the caper berry has no effect;
for the mere mortal is headed to his eternal home,
and mourners will walk around in the street;
6 before the silver cord is snapped,
and the gold bowl is broken,
and the jar is shattered at the spring,
and the wheel is broken into the well;
7 and the dust returns to the earth as it once was,
and the spirit returns to God who gave it.

This passage consists of poetry, warning a young person of the trials of growing old.

Under the sun. Now that I'm older, I understand some of the images in this poem. My muscles and tendons ache. My vision is not as crisp as it used to be, and my wife says I'm not hearing things as well.

The Teacher warned a young person to remember what God requires before the adversity of old age sets in.[6] Many commentators identify the various images in the poem with parts of the body that decline in old age, but their interpretations vary.[7] The poem ends with the reminder that in death, the body turns to dust and the spirit (or breath) returns to God.

I'm aware of my Creator now more than ever. I live under the sun.

In the Kingdom. The faith of a child is a reminder to the adults. The insight of a new believer is often applicable to a mature one.

I have written to you, children,
because you have come to know the Father.
I have written to you, fathers,
because you have come to know
the one who is from the beginning.
I have written to you, young men,
because you are strong,

---

[6]Shaw, pp. 150–152.
[7]Wright, pp. 1192–1194.

God's word remains in you,
and you have conquered the evil one.

1 John 2:14 (CSB)

John's letter includes encouragement for each level of maturity in the faith: new believers, mature ones, and in between. The new believers had established a personal relationship with God. The mature believers had an in-depth understanding of God's ways. The "young men" had learned the Word of God and had overcome attacks of Satan.

A typical local church has families with members of various ages. Similarly, that church has believers at various levels of spiritual maturity. They all need to hear and apply the Word of God, and they help each other grow. I live in the Kingdom.

16

Epilogue

If much of what happens is vanity, what can a guy do? What has lasting value in life?

Ecclesiastes 12:8 (CSB)

---

8 "Absolute futility," says the Teacher. "Everything is futile."

This verse introduces the Epilogue by repeating the phrases of 1:2 in the Prologue. If life under the sun is vanity, how do I live in the Kingdom?

[Jesus said to the crowd:] Those of you who do not give up everything you have cannot be my disciples.

Luke 14:33 (NIV)

Becoming a disciple who lives in the Kingdom, requires a commitment that takes priority over everything else.

As a young man, I had read the gospels and I wanted to be a disciple like Peter, James, and John. Then I was confronted by this verse. How much is everything? How do I give it up in the middle of a God-given career?

Proverbs

A clever proverb makes it easy to remember its nugget of wisdom.

Ecclesiastes 12:9–11 (CSB)

---

9 In addition to the Teacher being a wise man, he constantly taught the people knowledge; he weighed, explored, and arranged many proverbs. 10 The Teacher sought to find delightful sayings and write words of truth accurately. 11 The sayings of the wise are like cattle

prods, and those from masters of collections are like firmly embedded nails. The sayings are given by one Shepherd.

The beginning of this passage is marked by the personal action, "he constantly taught the people."

Under the sun. If Solomon were alive today, I wonder if he would write slogans for t-shirts and bumper stickers. A clever piece of wisdom on the back of
a car catches my attention at a stop light.

The Prologue says the Teacher applied wisdom to search for lasting value in
life. The Epilogue says he diligently acquired wisdom from anyone who spoke
wise proverbs. Wise sayings help one stay on the right path like prods guide
cattle, and help keep life together like nails. Certainly, one should remember
the teachings of the wise.

The book of Proverbs in the Bible is like a treasury. Solomon was the author
of much of the book of Proverbs. The proverbs there give me insight into human nature, handling money, responding to authority, and relating to people.
I live under the sun.

In the Kingdom. Ever since I became a believer, I have studied the Bible. Sometimes it gives me insight. Sometime it reveals my sinful patterns. Sometimes it
explains what righteousness really is. When I apply it to my life, I'm ready to
do good for others instantly.

All Scripture is inspired by God and is profitable for teaching, for
rebuking, for correcting, for training in righteousness, so that the
man of God may be complete, equipped for every good work.
2 Timothy 3:16–17 (CSB)

The Bible is the source of godly wisdom. It guides a believer in righteousness through teaching, rebuking, correcting, and training. Then the believer is
prepared to do good works.

The Bible shows me what Kingdom living is all about. I will embrace its
lessons. I live in the Kingdom.

Making books

In Solomon's time, books were written by hand. Block printing made printing multiple copies easier after the block was carved. Gutenberg's invention of
movable type made mass production of books practical. Computers and elec-
tronic media have made it possible to distribute information around the world
instantly and practically for free.

Ecclesiastes 12:12 (CSB)

---

12 But beyond these, my son, be warned: there is no end to the making of many books, and much study wearies the body.

This passage is further advice about seeking wisdom.

Under the sun. Thousands of new books are published every year. Even in a narrow field of study, the pile of books is overwhelming.

The Teacher's warning refers to making books of proverbs mentioned in the previous passage. The Teacher had personally experienced the weariness of much study.

After working in academia, I concur with the Teacher's warning. Much study will result in burn out. I live under the sun.

In the Kingdom. Studying the explanations of Bible scholars helps me avoid doctrinal mistakes. When scholars disagree, I have to be careful how I interpret a passage.

> Study to shew thyself approved unto God, a workman that needeth not to be ashamed, rightly dividing the word of truth.
> 2 Timothy 2:15 (KJV)

Paul recommended study to Timothy, so that his life would be commended by God. His study would give him understanding of God's Word, so he would not fall into heresy.

When I listen to preaching, I carefully consider whether the message conforms to the whole of God's Word. Heresy is sometimes subtle. In recent years, I have been taking "slow walks" as I meditate verse by verse. Sometimes I study a topic, using a concordance. Various study methods help me have a well rounded understanding. I live in the Kingdom.

Conclusion

Did did the Teacher succeed in his quest for lasting value in life?

Ecclesiastes 12:13–14 (CSB)

---

13 When all has been heard, the conclusion of the matter is this: fear God and keep his commands, because this is for all humanity [the whole duty of humanity]. 14 For God will bring every act to judgment, including every hidden thing, whether good or evil.

This passage is the conclusion of the entire book of Ecclesiastes. In verse 13, a CSB footnote gives an alternative translation of *for all humanity* as *the whole duty of humanity*. The end is marked by God's action.

Under the sun. Even as a little kid, I was aware of God's sovereignty over this world. Life under the sun is not the path of atheism. The Psalmist said, "The fool says in his heart, 'There is no God.' "[1]

The Teacher recommended enjoying life under the sun many times in Ecclesiastes, but most of all, he recommended fearing God and keeping his commands. His conclusion was not limited to ancient Israelites. It is for all humanity. As he said before, don't forget that God will judge everyone's actions.

The wise recognize God's sovereignty, so I will, too. I live under the sun.

In the Kingdom. When I think about how God has forgiven my sins because he loves me, it is easy to love him in return. When I think about how God loves every human being, it is easier to love those I encounter, too.

> [A Pharisee asked,] "Teacher, which command in the law is the greatest?"
>
> [Jesus] said to him, "Love the Lord your God with all your heart, with all your soul, and with all your mind. This is the greatest and most important command. The second is like it: Love your neighbor as yourself. All the Law and the Prophets depend on these two commands."
>
> Matthew 22:36–40 (CSB)

Jesus pointed out that the most important commandments in the Old Testament are love God and love your neighbor. These same commands are important for modern believers. The Teacher knew these commandments, so Jesus confirmed his advice.

People sin. Some say offensive things. Some have cranky attitudes. I don't love sinful actions, words, or attitudes, but I must look past actions, words, and attitudes to love the person.

> Then I saw a great white throne and one seated on it. Earth and heaven fled from his presence, and no place was found for them. I also saw the dead, the great and the small, standing before the throne, and books were opened. Another book was opened, which is the book of life, and the dead were judged according to their works by what was written in the books. Then the sea gave up the dead that were in it, and death and Hades gave up the dead that were in them; each one was judged according to their works.
>
> Revelation 20:11–13 (CSB)

---

[1] Psalm 14:1.

The New Testament confirms the Teacher's warning about judgment. This passage depicts a vision of the final judgment of mankind after Jesus returns. In this vision, the book of life recorded those whose sins are forgiven because of their faith. The other books recorded what had been done. Everyone was judged based on what he had done.

My name is in the book of life, so God's throne of judgment is not intimidating. I live in the Kingdom.

17

In the Kingdom

The Teacher's quest was to find lasting value in life. He asked a rhetorical question.

> What does a person gain for all his efforts that he labors at under the sun? Ecclesiastes 1:3 (CSB)
>
> Ecclesiastes 1:3 (CSB)

The book of Ecclesiastes answers, "All is vanity."[1]

Wisdom is inadequate

The Teacher used his wisdom to examine many aspects of life. He compared the lifestyles and characteristics of wisdom and folly. He tested the pleasure of accomplishments and the satisfaction of work. He presented many proverbs and insights to guide life.

> I applied my mind to examine and explore through wisdom all that is done under heaven... I have seen all the things that are done under the sun and have found everything to be futile, a pursuit of the wind.
>
> Ecclesiastes 1:13–14 (CSB)

Observation, experience, and logical reasoning were the Teacher's tools for his quest. However, his wisdom was inadequate to find lasting value in life under the sun.

A citizen of the Kingdom of God does not rely on intellect. Faith is the way to find lasting value in life.

---

[1] 1:2 (KJV) and 12:8 (KJV).

Now without faith it is impossible to please God, since the one who draws near to him must believe that he exists and that he rewards those who seek him.

Hebrews 11:6 (CSB)

Lasting value comes when one pleases God. The way to do that is through a personal relationship with him. This is available to everyone, not just the wise. The foundation of life in the Kingdom is faith. I live under the sun and in the Kingdom.

Fools and sinners

The Teacher observed fools in many situations. Fools despise wisdom. They always get in trouble. They take foolish risks. They say foolish things. They would rather party than work.

He also observed sin in society and its victims. He saw corrupt judges and government officials, and justice delayed. He saw oppression, jealousy, hasty vows, and greed.

And I realized that there is an advantage to wisdom over folly, like the advantage of light over darkness.

The wise person has eyes in his head,
but the fool walks in darkness.

Ecclesiastes 2:13–14 (CSB)

Foolishness and sin are vanity. Fools will be foolish, and sinners will sin. Even though being wise is not the way to lasting value in life, wisdom and common sense are better than foolishness and sin.

But know this: Hard times will come in the last days. For people will be lovers of self, lovers of money, boastful, proud, demeaning, disobedient to parents, ungrateful, unholy, unloving, irreconcilable, slanderers, without self-control, brutal, without love for what is good, traitors, reckless, conceited, lovers of pleasure rather than lovers of God, holding to the form of godliness but denying its power. Avoid these people.

2 Timothy 3:1–5 (CSB)

Paul warned Timothy that sin will run rampant in society the closer we get to Jesus' return. Sin is expressed in many ways. A citizen of the Kingdom recognizes sin for the evil it is, and avoids its snares. I live under the sun and in the Kingdom.

Everyone dies

The Teacher observed nothing one accomplishes yields lasting value under the sun after one dies.[2]

> Everything is the same for everyone: There is one fate for the righteous and the wicked, for the good and the bad, for the clean and the unclean, for the one who sacrifices and the one who does not sacrifice. As it is for the good, so also it is for the sinner; as it is for the one who takes an oath, so also for the one who fears an oath. This is an evil in all that is done under the sun: there is one fate for everyone.
>
> Ecclesiastes 9:2–3 (CSB)

No one escapes death. One's status in society does not matter. One's religiosity does not matter. One's morality does not matter. Everyone dies.

Even though everyone dies a natural death,[3] citizens of the Kingdom have the promise of resurrection when Jesus returns.

> The trumpet will sound, and the dead [in Christ] will be raised incorruptible, and we will be changed. For this corruptible body must be clothed with incorruptibility, and this mortal body must be clothed with immortality. When this corruptible body is clothed with incorruptibility, and this mortal body is clothed with immortality, then the saying that is written will take place:
>
> > Death has been swallowed up in victory.
> > Where, death, is your victory?
> > Where, death, is your sting?
>
> The sting of death is sin, and the power of sin is the law. But thanks be to God, who gives us the victory through our Lord Jesus Christ!
>
> 1 Corinthians 15:52–57 (CSB)

Because Jesus rose from the dead, believers will also be resurrected. Victory over death belongs to all who have entered the Kingdom through faith in Jesus. I live under the sun and in the Kingdom.

Enjoy life

Each time the Teacher searched for lasting value under the sun, he found only vanity. After such disappointments, what could he do?

---

[2] 2:11.
[3] Hebrews 9:27.

> There is nothing better for a person than to eat, drink, and enjoy his work. I have seen that even this is from God's hand, because who can eat and who can enjoy life apart from him?
>
> Ecclesiastes 2:24–25 (CSB)

The Teacher saw that enjoying the basics of life under the sun was the best outcome he could find. Over and over he recommended enjoying food, drink, and work. He also recognized that enjoyment of life under the sun is a gift from God. Those in the Kingdom respond with thanksgiving.

> For the kingdom of God is not eating and drinking, but righteousness, peace, and joy in the Holy Spirit.
>
> Romans 14:17 (CSB)

Life in the Kingdom is not about eating kosher food. Life in the Kingdom means abundant righteousness, peace, and joy in one's soul. I live under the sun and in the Kingdom.

God will judge

The Teacher emphasized over and over that God will hold each person accountable for what he has done.

> For God will bring every act to judgment, including every hidden thing, whether good or evil.
>
> Ecclesiastes 12:14 (CSB)

This last verse of Ecclesiastes is what the Teacher wanted readers to remember. God will judge. When will God enforce this accountability?

> When the Son of Man comes in his glory, and all the angels with him, then he will sit on his glorious throne. All the nations will be gathered before him, and he will separate them one from another, just as a shepherd separates the sheep from the goats.
>
> Matthew 25:31–32 (CSB)

When Jesus returns, he will reign as king and righteous judge. Judgment is guaranteed.[4] Everyone will be judged.[5] Believers will receive eternal life. Jesus knows who is a citizen of the Kingdom. I live under the sun and in the Kingdom.

---

[4] Hebrews 9:27.
[5] Revelation 20:11–13.

Obey the Creator

After considering all, the Teacher reached his conclusion: obey the Creator.

> When all has been heard, the conclusion of the matter is this: fear God and keep his commands, because this is [the whole duty of humanity].
>
> Ecclesiastes 12:13 (CSB)

Even though the Teacher did not find lasting value under the sun, he recognized that obeying the Creator is what mankind should do. Which commands are most important?

> [A Pharisee asked,] "Teacher, which command in the law is the greatest?"
>
> [Jesus] said to him, "Love the Lord your God with all your heart, with all your soul, and with all your mind. This is the greatest and most important command. The second is like it: Love your neighbor as yourself. All the Law and the Prophets depend on these two commands."
>
> Matthew 22:36–40 (CSB)

The Teacher was familiar with the two greatest commands of the Law, love God and love your neighbor. Jesus pointed out that the rest of the Law flows from these two. Life in the Kingdom means obeying these commands. A life of faith and a personal relationship with God makes such obedience practical. Jesus also gave his disciples a new command.

> I give you a new command: Love one another. Just as I have loved you, you are also to love one another. By this everyone will know that you are my disciples, if you love one another.
>
> John 13:34–35 (CSB)

Jesus loves us, so he sacrificed himself on the cross. As a citizen of the Kingdom, I must love other believers with self-sacrificing love. I live under the sun and in the Kingdom.

In the Kingdom

The Teacher sought lasting value in life under the sun. He found applying wisdom to life has good results, but does not have the lasting value he sought. He recommended obeying the Creator, but did not realize that faith in God results in eternal life, and that pleasing God gives purpose and meaning to life.

Do not be conformed to this age, but be transformed by the renew-
ing of your mind, so that you may discern what is the good, pleasing, and perfect will of God.

Romans 12:2 (CSB)

Life in the Kingdom renews one's mind, so one can discern God's will and
what pleases him. Doing what pleases him throughout my day stores treasure
in heaven—the lasting value the Teacher was seeking.

And whatever you do, in word or in deed, do everything in the
name of the Lord Jesus, giving thanks to God the Father through
him.

Colossians 3:17 (CSB)

A disciple's every action is done as a representative of Jesus. Even routine,
boring activities under the sun are done in his name. I'm free to love others;
I'm free to worship in my heart; and I'm free to be thankful while I'm doing
things under the sun.

My every action, word, and thought done under the sun is also done in
Kingdom when my motivation and my attitude are submitted to the lordship
of Jesus. I live under the sun and in the Kingdom.

. . . .
Please write a brief review of this book and post it at your on-line bookstore(s).

If you want to receive a weekly devotional meditation, please send your email
address to me at
edward.allen1949@gmail.com
Your email will not be used for any other purpose.

— Ed

Index

About the author

Edward B. Allen is the author of these books in daily devotional format.

- *A Slow Walk through Psalm 119: 90 Devotional Meditations*
- *A Slow Walk with James: 90 Devotional Meditations*
- *A Slow Walk with Peter: 275 Devotional Meditations*, including meditations on Jude
- *A Slow Walk during Christmas and Easter: Devotional Meditations for Advent and Lent*, including a chronological paraphrase of the Scriptures

He is also the author of these other books which are straight reads with a devotional slant.

- *The Kingdom of Heaven: A Devotional Commentary on the Discourses of Jesus in Matthew*
- *Revelation: A Devotional Commentary*, including illustrations by Albrecht Dürer, fifteen meditations, and questions for personal or group study
- *Under the Sun and in the Kingdom: A Devotional Commentary on Ecclesiastes*
- *Love, Sex, Money, and Power: A Devotional Commentary*, including twelve meditations
- *Honest Questions: A Personal Commentary on Genesis 1 through 11*

He has led discussion Bible-study groups in evangelical churches for over 45 years, and has authored devotional articles for *The Upper Room* and *The Secret Place* magazines. He received a Ph.D. in Computer Science degree at Florida Atlantic University. He has had a career in software engineering and has authored or coauthored over 80 professional papers.

Made in the USA
Middletown, DE
11 June 2023

32415481R00073